A bottle of wine contains more philosophy
than all the books in the world.

Louis Pasteur

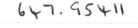

First published by Fledgling Press, 2011
This edition published by Fledgling Press, 2012

www.fledglingpress.co.uk

Cover design by Graeme Clarke

Printed in Great Britain by
www.berforts.co.uk
Stevenage

ISBN: 9781905916535

## Acknowledgements

This is usually where an author gratefully thanks all and sundry who have aided and abetted them in their pursuit of recognition – **NO WAY!** We did it all by ourselves so we'll take the credit, thank you very much.

Linda & Kate

# Foreword

Life Behind Bars is the brain child of two larger than life ex-pub landladies, Kate and Linda, who have been best friends for over thirty years and have racked up almost as many years collectively in the licensed trade.

Between them, they have owned and managed everything from a lap-dancing bar to an old country inn, and many others in between. Being a landlady is almost a vocation. You have to be all things, to all men, at all times. All that for probably fifty pence an hour. They have been threatened, they have been physically attacked and even shot at, and that was just family and friends. Wait till you hear what the customers get up to!

Join them on a hilarious journey meeting Tint Eastwood, the Three Marys, the Cider Man, The One Armed Bandit, Lily and Marion and many more, all with tales to tell.

Truth is often said to be stranger than fiction, and in this case it is hard to believe that many of these antics actually happened. But they did. All the names of the participants in this book have been changed by necessity; we don't want anyone being sued. Although there are a few we would dearly like to! Anyone who has ever run a pub or frequented one will immediately recognise the characters. In fact, it could be you we are writing about! Or maybe you are in the next one!

Sadly, in a few years there may well be no characters like Linda and Kate. Why? The rate of pub closures has reached epidemic levels. It is estimated that thirty pubs a week close - *thirty a week!* At that rate the 'Great British Pub' and the 'Great British Publican,' but more importantly the 'Great British Customer' will soon no longer exist.

This edition has all the old favourites from our first book and some new ones too. We hope you enjoy this book as much as readers tell us they enjoyed the first one.

# Life Behind Bars:
## Confessions of a Pub Landlady

## Late Night Lock-In Edition

# How do you do?

This is the tale of two formidable ex-landladies, who fear nothing and no one, except perhaps the VAT inspector and even he came to grief at their hands (honestly he did).

If we had a pound for every time a well meaning person uttered those immortal words 'You should write a book,' we could solve the National Debt. So we did; (write a book that is, not solve the National Debt) and here it is, so sit back and enjoy the ride.

I'm Linda and the senior of us two; obviously I don't look it. And I am wholly responsible for my partner in crime, otherwise known as Kate, becoming a member of that once elite body 'The Licensed Trade'.

I have always been the most generous of people, especially with pain and suffering, and she had avoided marriage very successfully so I saw no reason to let her off scot-free. I persuaded her to come and join us, and buy a pub. To let you know what a devoted friend I am, the night before her final interview with the brewery, I helped her demolish a litre bottle of vodka. Well you have to, don't you?

How she ever got through that I'll never know, but she did and she was off and running. I have to say she would have been better off running!

Within four weeks she had signed on the dotted line and paid her money. She was 'official' and 'legal'. This allowed her to sign passport applications and assure HMG that she had known most of the lowlifes in the area for at least ten years and they were of good standing! Apart from that there were no real advantages except that she could sell booze.

I generously offered to be her mentor and she would be my apprentice. That lasted exactly one hour. We had been friends for thirty years and had seldom had a cross word. Forty minutes into her new career she very unpleasantly told me she would dispense with my services and I was to 'fuck off' back to my own pub and leave her alone. Well!

As I said earlier, countless people had told us to write a book and countless times the reply had been, "If we did, you'd never believe it."

All the incidents have some bearing on the truth and all the characters have no bearing on reality, they are all real; just have no bearing on reality.

# You must be joking . . .

It is almost 2am and I am alone in the bar, lovingly nursing a delicious vodka and tonic and pondering over the evening's events. I enjoy the stillness of the place that less than an hour ago was bursting with life and noise, while the glasses remain strewn across the bar and the smell of cheap perfume and sweat still lingers. And the dog has piddled against the bar because you either forgot or ignored its plaintive barking to go out.

This is the world that we publicans inhabit and quite frankly, customers, in general, are a bloody nuisance and only make the place untidy. I would much prefer them just to send us a cheque once a week; we'd then supply them with booze delivered to their home and let the buggers mess up their lounges, be sick in their toilets and shag their own wives. How pleasant and profitable life would be.

But till that happens I can enjoy the solitude, until the phone breaks my reverie. All pub phones ring at a hundred decibels so they can be heard over the Saturday night noise. But at 2 am in an empty bar, it could summon the dead. So I struggle off a wobbly bar stool, (well I think it's the stool that's wobbling), wondering who has lost their keys, their mobile phone, or maybe a husband MIA.

"Hello?"

"Hello it's me."

"For fuck's sake, it's 2am which *me* is it?"

"It's *me*, me"

Then the penny dropped.

"What's wrong? What's happened?"

"Oh my God! Oh my God! You'll never guess! Big Agnes dropped down dead."

"You're kidding!" (Why anyone says this, or why anyone would joke about such a thing is beyond me.)

"Of course I'm not kidding. Oh my God it was terrible. We've had the police, ambulance, fire brigade. We even had to shut the bar early; lost a fucking fortune." (Oh yes, we are all that crass!)

"What happened?"

"Christ, you'll never believe it and if you laugh I will NEVER speak to you again."

God it *was* serious.

"What happened?"

"She dropped down dead."

"Dead?"

"Don't you laugh."

You should never say that to anyone. Even if it's not funny, they are going to roll about hysterically. I could feel the laughter rising already and I didn't know what had happened.

"Well she dropped down dead. Right at the end."

"The End?  End of WHAT?"

"You dare laugh!  Her song."

"For fuck's sake, her song?  She was singing?"

"Remember we had a big karaoke competition on."

"Right, right, and what happened?"

"Well Agnes had just come to the end, given it full blast, grand finale and then she just dropped down, stone cold dead.  Oh my God, I still can't believe it."

Why would she think I'd laugh, what could be remotely funny about that?  There's more to this!

"What was she singing?" I whispered.

"I knew it, I knew you'd twig!"

You know what's coming?  You've already guessed?  What would I twig?  What was she singing?  Yes folks, it was:

*I WILL SURVIVE*

"Hello?  Are you there?  Linda?  Hello, hello?"

# Happy Birthday . . .

It had looked like it was going to be a really good night. We had a 50<sup>th</sup> birthday party booked. The family, who were good, regular customers, had been decorating the lounge all afternoon and it was spectacular. There were masses of helium balloons, streamers and party poppers everywhere. I knew the cleaner would go fecking ballistic in the morning and demand double time, but hey ho!

The sandwiches were cut, but not curled! No one had burned the sausage rolls and we managed to get the cat's teeth marks off the chicken drumsticks. Guests were arriving bearing gifts, all well scrubbed and ready to party. I had no misgivings about this crowd as I knew them well. Maybe I took my eye off the ball a little, and gave them the benefit of the doubt. Not clever, there was BOOZE involved.

The karaoke was belting out the old favourite *I Did it My Way* sung by the latest Frank Sinatra wannabe! Shame she hadn't shaved and changed her socks. Drinks were flowing, tills were ringing and I was in the kitchen cutting the birthday cake when I was suddenly aware of the silence; that eerie silence when all you can hear is the music from 'High Noon' ringing in your ears.

The two adversaries had been staring in silence at each other for the past three hours; not a word had been spoken. Many, many years previously, in fact probably at the 21$^{st}$ birthday party, one had inadvertently spilled the other's drink and committed the cardinal sin of not 'getting them in again'. Sacrilege in a Scots pub.

Suddenly one of the two jumped up, stared malevolently into the other's face and with the battle-cry of the wronged –

"Aw, fuck it!" – he knocked the other clean out.

Then the party really began, tables, chairs, drinks, handbags and hair extensions went up in the air, and all the while the karaoke belting out 'Send in the Clowns.' Sometimes I just give up!

"Great party!" shouts one wit as I propelled him bodily out into the night air.

It looked like a scene from the O.K. Corral and the Indians had gained more than a few scalps. The birthday boy was under a pile of chairs snoring his head off, dead to the world. He was loaded onto a 'legless table' by a couple of his 'legless relations' and carted off.

"SAY GOODBYE TO THE DEPOSIT!" I roared after them.

"Cheers, hen, brilliant night! See ya tomorrow."

Bloody numbskulls. And then spying the DJ, I let him have it too. "SHUT THE FUCK UP and pack your gear away ya eejit. The party's over and don't think you're getting paid either!"

While this was happening the bar was full to bursting with all the local neds who had missed the action and perhaps felt a little cheated; after all it was Saturday night and it wasn't a good Saturday without a good fight. And they didn't consider that to be a good fight.

No blood, no stitches, only a couple of broken chairs and the karaoke machine still intact. (Average life span of a karaoke machine in a town bar was six months.)

So round two was about to kick off. However, they hadn't reckoned with me. I was absolutely spitting mad, dancing with temper. When calm, I am a force to be reckoned with, but in full sail and ready for action; more dangerous than a caged cougar!

I studied the group for approximately thirty seconds and they studied me. Bearing in mind most had double vision by now; I must have looked like a mob! I moved in on the ringleader, who was backing hastily towards the door, all the while making wisecracks just to keep face.

Should I cut him off at the pass? Or just go for it? The staff were waiting with baited breath, ready to spring to my aid, *my* aid! I don't think so! One snarl, just one snarl, that's all it took, bit of an anti-climax actually and the bar was empty. Disaster had been averted, well for us anyway.

Poor Tony the Chippie had the remains of the birthday party and the neds in a face-off. He lost a plate glass window and his beautiful shiny red formica tables never stood properly upright again.

# Whys and Wherefores . . .

"Why a pub? A pub? Why the devil do you want to work in a pub? You've got a great life."

My mother was appalled, she couldn't believe we would willingly give up 'the company life' for what she called 'going into service.' My husband, on the other hand, was over the moon; free booze for life and he wouldn't have to leave the comfort of home. Those sentiments should have been a chilling warning for me.

David was never a good drinker. Oh, he wasn't violent or aggressive, in fact, the complete opposite. He was a lovely drunk, lovely to everyone else. He just didn't know when to stop and invariably was sent off to bed, or home early at any party. Not a problem in our previous life but every night was party night in a pub. Be careful what you wish for, it might just come true.

I have to say my mother was right, we did have a great life. David worked for the French Merchant Navy, had a great job (took him away from home!) We lived in a very affluent and sociable village and our daughter was just about to go off to college. But I always resented the fact that all the profits we were making went to the company and I couldn't see why we shouldn't make money for ourselves. Our first venture should have put us off for life but . . . always the eternal optimist.

We had had our offer on a town bar accepted. We were over the moon and couldn't wait to get started. For reasons I never discovered there was a hiccup with the contract. We were due to go off on holiday for a week and having a very pedantic lawyer, she would not let us sign. I was so disappointed and actually quite annoyed at the situation. I was sure we were going to lose it and someone else would jump in and buy it from under us. The present incumbent had been trying to offload it for over a year but that didn't stop me from panicking.

We arrived home late one Sunday evening and there were literally dozens of messages asking us to contact the brewery, the lawyer and God knows who else. So first thing Monday morning I dropped David off at work and drove past the pub. It looked different but I couldn't quite figure out why. I drove about fifty yards further on and screeched to a halt. There was no fucking roof! No roof! What the hell had happened?

Well, unfortunately no one had informed the 'Drug Baron', to whom Mr. Seller owed thousands, that there was a new sheriff in town! Me. Thank God the lawyer was as strict as she was.

We would have had no insurance, no building and no money.  Looking back it was the biggest favour anyone has ever done us but at the time it was devastating.

It was time to circle the wagons and strategise; never really understood what that meant but it sounded good.  There had to be a pub out there with our name on it.  I was going to find it and I was going to make it work!  And I did, and it did.

# Confused? . . . You will be . . .

Tea-time drunks are normally the funniest, usually the least aggressive, but positively the most confused. They have no conception of time because they have spent the afternoon in a warm, dim cocoon being cosseted by a buxom young filly, tending to their every need. Then they emerge into bright sunlight and are absolutely baffled. It should be dark, close to midnight. So it often makes for amusing antics.

In Tweedy's we had two entrances, (or exits), which for one old geezer proved completely baffling. Staggering into the public bar for what looked like his tenth 'one for the road', I politely informed him he would not be served and sent him on his merry way. This reception is never met with good grace, after all "Who the fuck am I to say he's had enough?" And this gent was no exception. Muttering the usual pleasantries under his breath, he headed for the next hostelry, where he would surely be met with open arms and delight.

Instinctively I knew he would follow the neon sign, so I nipped across the hall as he fell through the lounge door. Seeing me behind the bar came as something of a shock but he didn't argue, just about turned and fell back through the door. By now his bearings were completely off and he was like the 'Bisto Kid' following his nose, and of course he was heading back the way he'd come.

With the greatest effort he carefully opened the bar door. He was taking no chances; well he'd just been refused in two pubs. Drawing himself up to his full 5 feet, he walked as steadily as he could up to the bar with that look of 'nearly home and dry', saw me and roared.

"For fuck's sake! How many pubs have you got in this toon?" and promptly passed out.

We propped him up in a corner and he slept almost through till closing time, probably the latest he's been out on the town for years. When he woke he thanked us profusely for a 'great night' and he would see us tomorrow.

I don't think so!

# Through the looking glass . . .

It was definitely a full moon tonight. Every eejit in the town had passed through my doors and each one dafter than the one before; not causing trouble, just plain, bloody stupid. I was looking forward to a large G&T and putting my feet up. Landladies have a sixth sense about customers and we can sense an atmosphere quicker than 'a rat up a drain pipe,' and tonight it was okay. All the loonies had moved on or were baying at the moon. I was sure I could make my escape early, but I'd give it just ten more minutes.

We had a policy of not allowing anyone in after 11pm unless I was very sure of them. I spotted one such buck who had been in earlier in the evening but had gone off to meet friends in town. He was somewhat the worse for wear but he was a good lad and always full of fun. Tonight, however, he was taking ages to come to the bar and seemed to be getting agitated with someone standing at the fireplace.

Watching for several minutes I decided I should intervene as Billy was now becoming over-excited and several other customers were unsure of him.

Although normally good natured, he was certainly in a lather about something. As I approached him cautiously (he's a big chap), he turned and grabbed me in a bear hug.

"Oh, Kate, Kate. For God's sake! What the fuck's wrong with everyone? I've been trying to get a drink for the past ten minutes and that bastard behind the bar is just taking the piss and making a fool of me."

"Don't you worry," says I, "he'll not be behind my bar again."

Yes, you've guessed, he was looking in the mirror!

# Taking care of business . . .

Serving alcohol comes with its own problems, the main one being, people get drunk. Having relieved them of their wits and their money, any good publican will look after their own drunks. We never, ever look after anyone else's. This rule should be tattooed on every member of staff's forehead.

Picture the scene: an extremely busy Friday night, the bar absolutely heaving and the staff were working at full speed. One stunning but ditzy barmaid, Claire, was gesturing to me she had to have a break. This meant I had to leave my stance as bouncer at the front door and take over in the bar.

As you have sussed by now, no one gets past me! I had spent the last fifteen minutes persuading a well-known drunk that coming in for a nightcap was not a good idea. He had eventually moved on and was gingerly feeling his way home but was definitely out of our radar. Feeling it was quite safe to leave Claire to her cigarette, I took her place behind the bar.

Imagine my horror when I spotted the idiot of a girl carefully negotiating her way back into the main body of the kirk with the bloody man on her arm.

"He's not feeling well," she mouthed to me.

"NOT FEELING WELL! *You'll* not be feeling well when I get out from behind this bar!"

She was intent on ministering to him and taking care of his needs because the poor man had to be ill, after all he could hardly stand. Hardly stand! Hardly walk; he was fucking legless! And we were lumbered with him. But not for long; in the flick of a barman's apron he was up and 'going for gold' in the only way a true drunk can.

'Head down and charge at the gate'. Only it was our fruit machine that got it. Everyone's a winner? He was knocked clean out and the punters thought it was raining pennies from heaven, only it was pound coins.

MY BLOODY POUND COINS

Guess who didn't get paid that week?

# Chucking out time . . .

During my career I have frequently operated two or three outlets at the same time. On one particularly busy Bank holiday I found myself, yet again, over-extended and short-staffed, hey ho! What's new?

On this occasion I had two major outlets. Both busy as hell and both needing my full attention (which is about that of a gnat!) And both short-staffed on an extremely busy Saturday.

I knew I could rely on a couple of the commis chefs to get me through the lunch period. On the promise of double time and a day off sometime, I managed to cover the Country Inn.

Tweedy's was the most popular venue in town and I would manage here on my own. The queue began to form at about 11.30am and by noon the place was heaving. I have to say, personally I wouldn't queue if Gordon Ramsay himself was frying the chips.

Anyway, usual Saturday, 250-300 lunches, and I have to say at the end of the shift, (actually any shift), I looked like someone had thrown the entire contents of the kitchen at me. I'm one messy cook. I had no time to change; jumped in the car, off to prep for the evening shift at the Country Inn, to feed another 250 starving punters.

How I managed to get through that day God alone knows. But at the end of a gruelling twelve hours I was absolutely done in. So back in the car, leaving my husband and manager in charge! Huh!

If I was a mess at 2pm, you can't imagine what I looked like at 9pm, absolutely appalling. First stop shower, second, a very large vodka and tonic.

As I was turning the key in the lock I could hear the phone ringing.

"Bugger off! I don't care who it is, I'll get them later."

Got to the top of the stairs and a voice from below shouts.

"Phone David NOW! There's a problem down the road."

For heaven's sake, I'd only left them ten minutes ago. What the hell could have happened in ten minutes?

An agitated David was roaring down the phone. "You have to get back here NOW. There's a crowd of bikers refusing to leave and demanding drinks in the restaurant."

Jesus! Bikers! Every warning bell went off.

"Can't you deal with them?"

"No, they won't move; it's causing a problem in the restaurant."

This was serious, people don't come out on a Saturday night to become involved in, or watch, bar room brawls. It had to be sorted. And with great macho men, a woman is always the one to get rid of them.

It normally took about ten minutes to go from one place to the other but I think I broke the sound barrier. I stormed into the building, crashing doors, screeching at customers to get out of my way. Now, anyone who knows me knows that although I'm formidable, I never lose my cool. Well this was an exception.

No sign of hubby or manager. I marched through the dining room. No sign of any marauding hoards of leather-clad fiends. I spotted a group of about eight to ten extremely boisterous lads by the pool table. No obvious clues that they were bikers, but who knows? They could be in their civvies. Well they were out, whether they knew it or not.

I marched up, lifted all their drinks, of which there were many, and threw them on the bar. Grabbed a couple by the scruff of the neck and propelled them to the door. Grabbing the next two wasn't as easy as the element of surprise had gone, but come hell or high water they were going.

To say they were protesting is putting it mildly. They were shouting and jumping up and down and going to smash the windows. Anyway, I got the last one, who was snogging the ugliest of uglies, (actually did him a favour), and dragged him screaming to the door to join the rest of his cohorts.

This was accomplished in approximately three minutes. Once a punter is outside it's easier to deal with them; you just shut the door. And that was what I was about to do when the dynamic duo appeared. The two of them stood open-mouthed at what I thought was my speed and dexterity in dealing with the situation.

"Who the fuck are they?" yelled the manager.

"The troublemakers," was my reply.

"Troublemakers? Why? What were they doing?"

"I don't know! You damned well called me."

"For fuck's sake! It's not them! It's *them*!"

"Who? *Them*?"

Having taken up residence at the vacant pool table was a group of elderly gentlemen.

"*THEM*? You're having a laugh."

I'd risked life and limb to get back in record time. Thrown possibly a dozen young guys out on their necks for nothing, risking a bloody riot to deal with a group whose collective age would be about 400 years old – the youngest was definitely over 60!

"*Them*? You fucking well called me back here to deal with a SAGA tour? *THEM*?"

Meanwhile, the victims were creating mayhem. (All landladies are secret swearers, and what we utter under our breath is never said out loud, but not in this case.) I have members of staff who have worked for me for over twenty years and have never, ever, heard or seen me like I was that night.

I always say when I lose my sense of humour, run for the hills, and this was it. Those two fuckin' eejits were supposed to be in charge and attend to customers, see to their needs, or if any problems arose, deal with them.

It seemed that the group of gentlemen, who were on their annual 'Chapter Ride Out,' had not wanted to venture into the bar. It was a little too noisy and maybe a bit rough. These were the 'Hells Angels'?

And what about the young guys I'd thrown out? Well they were pacified by a couple of free drinks and the threat that if they caused any trouble, I would be back.

# Lock In . . .

Every manager or owner has one golden rule: check everywhere, *everywhere,* before you lock up for the night. There are hundreds of tales of customers being locked in pubs. So we all have a check-out system. Mine took the same route every night and the gent's cubicle was the scene of many macabre incidents. One in particular rises above all others.

It was the usual Saturday night, place jumping, and I finally got everyone out. It never fails to amaze me, that having worked a ten hour shift and listened to the crap that drunks think you'll find phenomenally interesting, they still expect you to be full of bonhomie at one o'clock in the morning and find it quite impertinent that you want them to drink up and leave. Bloody cheek! The law has nothing to do with this, it's personal!

Desperate for my bed, I carried out my last inspection. As I progressed through the bar I switched off lights but could still see clearly under the emergency system, except in the gents. To check in there involved a complicated contortion, standing on one leg, (honestly), while precariously stretching the other out as far as I could.

Why? Well the passage between the two doors leading into the gents had no emergency light and was therefore pitch black. Last thing; check cubicle. This particular night when I kicked the cubicle door it bounced back. It shouldn't have. On closer inspection there was a body.

Oh! Fuck, a dead one! Panic! Fear! Then a snore, thank God!

Problem was he was absolutely jammed solid between the toilet and the wall; he was a big boy. He had to be if I was able to tell from that angle! Jokes aside, I had to get him up and out. I pushed and pulled and smacked and thumped, to no avail. The only thing was to get help.

Now the majority of my customers were brilliant but to invite them back into the bar was asking for trouble. I'd never get the buggers out, but I had no choice. Charlie boy was well and truly stuck.

The fates were on my side. When I gingerly opened the door, there, in full snog, was Davie the plumber. Honestly, there he was, with about ten of his mates. I shouldn't have been surprised, he'd be in all night and drunk at least twenty pints. Wonder if he needed the loo? How was I going to capture him without the rest of them piling in thinking it was Christmas?

Just at that moment, their minibus arrived and to my absolute delight, Davie had succumbed to the charms of the snogger, waved off his pals and went back in for round two. Thank you Lord! I'll be a better person from now on. I immediately captured Davie, handed him a screwdriver – okay, so a plumber doesn't usually use one – and showed him my problem.

The screwdriver was needed after all. We had to unscrew the toilet, move it to the side, haul the inert lump out, and then screw it back down. Eventually we got the stupid bugger on his feet and got him mobile, grumbling all the while he had a pint somewhere.

"Fuck off!"

Now I just had to get rid of the plumber and the snogger. On the promise of a free lunch, they made their way blissfully home and I crawled into bed an hour later than intended.

Gives a new meaning to 'a lock in'.

# Jump for joy . . .

Forget bar skittles and dominoes, any good bar has its own signature game which can only be enjoyed after hours and when absolutely pissed.

Why? Because that's the rules!

Our particular game evolved one Sunday night when the staff and a few chosen customers were enjoying an extra drink after hours during one of those extremely intelligent conversations, which only occur after copious amounts of booze! And you never understand why no one has ever thought of it before. *Genius Rules!*

Squinting with one eye so he could focus, Jason issued the challenge; who could clear the length of the bar in the fewest jumps? Just like the hop, skip and jump in the Olympics.

Now I have to say, very few of us were built for jumping and I wasn't sure the bar would stand it. But they were all game and very soon everyone was getting into the swing of it. Bets were being taken and the best so far was five jumps.

We were making such a racket it was some time

before we realised there was a loud banging on the front door. I tried to quieten everyone down and went to answer it. 'After hours' was seriously frowned upon in the town and it was something we rarely indulged in, but there before me were two members of the local constabulary.

"We've had complaints about excessive noise coming from this establishment and must speak to the Licensee."

I showed them into the bar, just as Jason, beyond all control, was in mid-flight on jump number four.

"What's going on here?"

"It's a private party, officer."

"As you can see, no till."

This was always the landlord's 'Get out of Jail' card. No till meant you were not selling alcohol. It is not against the law to give it away. As if! It was the only time credit was ever allowed in this bar and everyone had to settle up before leaving.

"Look, we are so sorry, we didn't realise we were disturbing anyone and we'll stop right now."

"Oh no we won't!" yelled Jason . . .

He was now running full pelt down the bar, ready to launch himself into his jump. What happened next will go down in the annals of time. Just as he was about to take off, he stood on a discarded slice of lemon and literally did the splits the whole length of the bar. It makes your eyes water just thinking about it. Well, if he spoke with a falsetto voice before, he had now shot off the scale; developed a squint and a lisp! He walked with a limp too for many months.

Beating a hasty retreat the two officers left us with a stern warning and the promise of dire retribution if they had to return.

# Thieving buggers . . .

It seems the better you are as an employer, the more certain staff will abuse or disappoint you. Pubs are a blissful haven for the thief, usually because detection is difficult. I have had members of staff under surveillance by undercover cops and still they managed to avoid capture.

One in particular was so blatant that a number of regulars actually sent me an anonymous letter. They weren't concerned about my losses, just the fact that her husband was not paying his way and therefore having a free night at their expense.

It appeared that when it was this chap's time to buy a round, he ordered as usual, proffered no money, the drinks were made up and he even received £10 or so in change. Not a bad haul for the night, much to the chagrin of the rest of his cronies, who felt that what was sauce for the goose should be sauce for the rest of the flock. She of course was sacked and he was barred.

The annoying result was that I also lost his five mates as customers for a while.

Another scam which is prevalent in almost every bar

at some time is BYOB, just like they do at parties. Only here the barmaid/man will bring a bottle of their own cheap crap, decant it into a brand-name bottle and at the end of the shift, pocket the amount sold.

This keeps the landlord's stock correct and the miscreant can holiday in the Bahamas at our expense.

# Fill your boots . . .

Then we have the real professionals; usually staff you inherit and who have perfected their perks to 'perkfection'. These guys know every scam in the book. They are usually so plausible and the thought that they would steal so abhorrent that catching them is a nightmare.

I know a few who actually set newbies up as patsies for their crimes. Believe me, this was when they could make a killing.

One, who we will call Pat, was so indiscriminate in her thieving she actually had family members come in with bags to collect her haul. If she ran out of coffee at home she would scatter some on the kitchen floor and tell the duty manager she had dropped the tin and had to throw it all away. Seeing the mess on the floor who would doubt her?

She would blithely tell us she was inviting all her family to Sunday dinner; what she didn't say was that I would have the pleasure of paying for it! For an experienced cook, she burned a helluva lot of roast joints! This was my excuse for getting rid of her.

It was cheaper to close the kitchen than to maintain her lifestyle.

# Fingers in the Till

Naivety is no excuse for stupidity and most of us have been stupidly trusting, time and time again. Whilst I always had a good grip on drinks stocks, it was more difficult to check on food sales due to wastage etc. However I found myself in a position where no matter how knackered I was, and we equate being knackered with being busy, I always appeared to have the same takings.

"Fool!" I hear you cry, "Check the tabs!"

Truthfully, I never suspected for one minute someone was at the fiddle. Until it hit me smack in the face. Thieves can't allow for sick leave or emergencies. This particular thief would drag himself into work commendably, no matter how ill, or hungover, he was. I thought he was a Trojan! Little did I know the bastard was keeping two families and a girlfriend on the strength of my steak and ale pie.

However, there came a time when even he had to admit defeat and have a few days off. His poor old mother had died and, unbelievable though it may seem, he actually wanted to come into work that morning.

"No, no, no, you must take as much time off as you need."

For the first couple of days we were delighted at how much improved the lunchtime takings were, and had no suspicions. However, on the fourth day we were unusually quiet but still maintained the usual level of takings. Something was beginning to smell and it wasn't the fish.

Time to really investigate what was going on. Without alerting the other staff I did a full stocktake and checked all the till rolls. It seemed that he would ring up the bill, but with the till open, so it didn't properly register. Customer pays and thief simply cancels the sale. This was done on probably 20% of checks. Over a week? Not a bad bonus scheme. We later discovered that he was pocketing half the tips also. Now stealing from me is bad enough, but stealing from your workmates?

He resumed work on the Monday and I was ready for him. We balanced the number of kitchen tabs with the takings and I am utterly ashamed to admit the difference. The average he was pocketing could well afford to keep two families, two girlfriends and probably even a cat.

The bastard!! He nearly joined his mother!

# Ladies Choice . . .

Early on in our career, Saturday afternoons were never the busiest of times for us. Once the lunchtime crowd had gone, we were left with a few old faithfuls.

David came up with the idea of having Go-Go dancers for the dead time. 'You'll be freekin' dead if you try that caper,' I thought. Well, much to my disapproval two dancers were hired and word went out.

At 2.45pm there were two old geezers nursing a half Guinness. At 2.50pm there were two hundred heaving, heavy breathing numbskulls crammed into the bar. I have never seen anything like it. Okay, I thought, minimum £5.00 per drink. We literally took megabucks in that two hour period. The dancers would be a regular appearance from now on.

What surprised me more than anything was that they were generally great girls. One was studying for a BA in Divinity, another was the niece of a prominent member of the aristocracy who had fallen on hard times, and a few were single mums trying to make a crust. Of course there were the usual slappers amongst them and some were definitely a bit long in the tooth. One girl, Big Marie, one of the old brigade and certainly not in the first blush of youth, could really get the crowd going. She left nothing to the imagination!

Watching as she was getting ready to go on, I remarked she appeared to have put on a bit of weight since the last time she'd worked for us.

"Hey, Marie, been overdoing it a bit?"

"Just water retention," she replied.

The retention was cured two days later when her waters broke in Marks and Spencer's and she gave birth to a 6lb girl in the back of a black cab on the way to the Nursing Home.

She was back on stage two weeks later. Well, she did have an extra mouth to feed!

# Sweet smell of . . .

There are regulars and then there are regulars. Most publicans know their customers either by their tipple or their nickname. Very few actually know the names of individuals. We had the Cider Man, Old Dustin, Big Mary, Wee Mary and Anybody's Mary (work that one out). The Steak Pie Man, Dirty Gary and Snotter, and like most pubs, we had a Smelly Brigade; members of the great unwashed.

A very mixed bag, each of whom you had to drink down wind of, and preferably in the next bar, during the summer months. One of this ripe crowd, named Herbie, dressed in the most bizarre fashion. He looked like an Oxfam reject. He seldom changed; he just added another layer when the stains became too obvious. It was quite normal to see him wearing two shirts, a t-shirt and a couple of sweaters in the middle of July! Much to his delight, we clubbed together to buy him a new shirt for Christmas. He was so taken with the garment which we had carefully chosen to camouflage the food stains, that hard though this is to believe, he steadfastly refused to change it until just before Valentine's Day.

It went round like wild fire. Herbie's got a date. Well he had, and he appeared early in the evening with his usual mismatch of clothes and a 'new shirt' but the smell lingered on. On close inspection, (well as close as you would want to go), we discovered he had no *new* shirt; he had just turned his Christmas present inside out, honest! His date ventured halfway down the bar then beat a hasty retreat.

It puzzled me for weeks how he'd managed to snare the young woman in the first place. Until I sussed out he'd answered a Lonely Hearts Ad.

They had never actually met!

# Twin Set . . . and Match

There were two sets of twins in this group; a pair of each gender, although that was questionable. We had two women of an indeterminate age, tiny in stature and with ferocious tempers. They were such a peculiar pairing it was often remarked that in the case of one of them, they had mistakenly thrown out the baby and kept the 'afterbirth'.

They were a bit like a couple of Jack Russells who thought they were Dobermans and would ridiculously take on all-comers, no matter what size, sex or build, after just a couple of beers.

One was married and definitely suffered from O.C.D. The other was single and made Herbie smell like a bed of roses. Neither were the sharpest knives in the drawer but both had that weasel cunning and missed nothing. They were true exponents of the art of free drinks. Both could appear early in the day and be well-oiled by closing time, having spent virtually nothing. They were not real scroungers; they had just perfected the art.

However, by closing time they became a menace. They would circle the bar looking for a fight or an argument. They were two of the most aggressive drunks. If there were no other malevolent punters then they would fight each other. They would fight night after night, no winner, no loser, just regular visits to A & E.

They eventually ceased their patronage when the unmarried smelly one was sent down for three months. One of her equally odorous pals had won a holiday for two in sunny Spain.

Unfortunately, this prize could not be exchanged for cash, nor could anyone but the winner and a partner go, despite many telephone calls to the benefactors. So there was no option but to participate in a two week beano in Benidorm of sun, sea, and in their case, Sangria!

Presumably as the holidaymakers would have to share a room, there were very few takers. Hence twin number two struck gold. There was a problem! Due to the state of her home, no one would volunteer to look after her pets. She had the most ferocious little Yorkie that seldom saw daylight and a couple of goldfish.

Not to be done out of a holiday, the stupid bitch had opened a dozen tins of dog food, laid them out with two bowls of water, chucked some fish food in the tank and gone off for two weeks in the sun.

She should have got a lot longer than three months and been fed a diet of bread and water. More than the poor dog got.

# What the f f f f f f?

The other twins, Harry and Gerry, were as mad as a box of frogs and smelt equally as unpleasant. These guys were absolutely identical. However, there was one dead give-away. Harry had a terrible speech impediment. He had a severe stutter, and a very pronounced lisp. Sadly, they were of the generation where nothing had been done to help him overcome these problems. So 'any simple sentence' became:

"Tth th th tho    eh eh eh any    th th th thimple    th th th thentence."

This gruesome twosome were only allowed in at certain times for the sake of my other customers. They spent most of their barred time working out how to outwit us and gain entry. They seldom succeeded but were absolutely infuriating.

Like many twins they squabbled and bickered constantly, but poor Harry never won an argument because he was always three sentences behind. The madder he got the more pronounced his impediment became and he spent most of his time jumping up and down, screaming at the top of his lungs.

"F f f fucking, b b b bastard! I I I I'll, f f f fucking, k k k kill you! Y y y ya, f f f fucking, idiot!"

Or some other such pleasantries.

They were inveterate gamblers but unlike most they seemed to win more than they lost. There was one problem though, they were virtually illiterate and Harry could never be trusted to put on the bet. By the time he got the details out, the race was usually finished.

On one memorable occasion however, this worked to his advantage. He had been sent to put a fair sum of money on a horse called 'Fascinating Flirt' but it proved too difficult and after several attempts at 'f f f f f f' he changed the bet to a horse he could pronounce called 'Once in a While.'

Well you can imagine the reception he got from his brother, who was convinced his £100 was down the drain. On the brink of another battle, the race results came up on the TV and, lo and behold, 'Once in a While' won the race. The f f f fucking other h h h horse is probably still running . . .

Next to gambling, their other passion was Dean Martin; they were his greatest fans. Every day they would select a tune on the juke box and play it over and over again. I can't listen to Deano without a shudder and because of them we all dreaded Christmas.

Harry's rendition of 'Let It Snow, Let It Snow, Let It Snow' took till Easter!

# Date Night . . .

Jimmy was an associate of this crowd, a poor soul who at the age of 55 became a single father to two fairly young children. He had been in the Merchant Navy for years and had married fairly late in life. Unknown to him, his new wife was a closet alcoholic who managed to keep things on an even keel while Jimmy was at home. So he would go off to sea under the misapprehension that all was well.

When the children came along, things went from bad to worse and he had to weigh anchor and take over. Things got so bad he moved out with the children but stayed in constant contact with his wife. When she had money she would drink, when she had none the kids could visit.

This carried on for a few years and although it wasn't the best situation, it looked like it was working reasonably well. Until that fateful night she fell asleep with a cigarette in her hand and died in the ensuing fire.

Many people have a black sense of humour and I'm probably worse than most. So when I read the notice of her funeral, it struck me as excruciatingly funny. The family were taking no chances when they announced she would be cremated.

A few weeks later Jimmy appeared in the bar along with the kids and he had a large parcel which looked almost gift wrapped.

"Oh, Jimmy!" says I, "You shouldn't have bothered."

"It's the wife," he replied.

What could I say? Mind you, it was the first time they had been out together in years!

# If it's not nailed down . . .

Staff stealing is one thing but customers under the 'affluence of incohol' think most pubs are a free-for-all. We have had everything, including the bar cat, nicked at one time or another. Some eejit even took the goldfish out of the tank in his crash helmet. Fortunately for my poor wee fish we caught him at the door. The thief had more than a wet head, believe me. The cat, I think, was either a suicide attempt or just plain running away and I knew just how it felt.

But the most unusual and questionable piece to be stolen, on numerous occasions, was the gents toilet door. What anyone would want with a toilet door and especially the gents (ladies being slightly sweeter), is absolutely beyond me.

We would frequently receive a call from the local constabulary informing us that the door had been on its travels again and had turned up on someone's roof rack, outside the Scout Hut and even in the vestry of the church. Someone had actually pinned the order of service on it!

However, one evening in late October, off it went again never to return.  I must say that at the local bonfire on Guy Fawkes night there was the most pungent smell of ammonia, which leads me to believe . . .!

# Smoking Ban . . .

One memorable theft was so blatantly cheeky it almost had to be admired. Often on Sunday afternoon we would have a band playing in the bar and it would be particularly busy. The cigarette machine was usually located near the door in the bar and after one busy Sunday people had been complaining about the lack of a machine.

Towards the end of that week I called the company to ask when it was to be returned and was more than a little surprised when they informed me that they never took machines off-site, but either repaired or replaced them immediately. So it had been stolen.

Given that the machine had never been secured, just basically plugged in, I am surprised it hadn't gone earlier. But the culprits had removed it in broad daylight and carried it across our car park. No one ever admitted to seeing anything.

Mind you one particular brand of cigarettes with only eighteen in the packet was frequently passed round for weeks!

# What a Turkey . . .

New Year is without doubt the most celebrated holiday in Scotland and the only day we closed. It was the one day I could invite friends and family to dinner.

The Chef had lovingly prepared a huge stuffed turkey and a fantastic glazed ham, which would feed the dozen or so guests expected. I had spent a fortune on making sure everything was just right and was looking forward to our celebrations.

Hogmanay had been riotous as usual and the bar had been packed to capacity. Everyone having a great time. I vaguely remember someone asking if we had a large carrier bag and I'm sure one of the staff obliged.

Fuck me! We helped them to nick our dinner! If I had caught them it would have been their 'Last Supper!'

How to explain to my hungry guests that it was turkey flavoured crisps and pork scratchings but with all the trimmings for dinner . . .

I'm sure I'll laugh about it one day!

# Inside Job . . .

The piéce de resistance has to be the theft experienced by Hubby and Co. For a short while I had taken over a pub in town and at the end of the first week sent David, and Chic my cellar man, up to check on things.

David emptied the fruit machine and the safe and cleverly left the money bag on the windowsill in full view of the local neds. He then joined Chic in the cellar. He heard a crash but dismissed it as someone outside. Oh! They were outside alright – outside with my fucking takings!

He phoned in a panic, what was he to do?

"Well phone the police for a start."

I asked him how much he thought had been stolen. He reckoned about £1,000. Being the honest and upright citizen I am, I told him to say £1250 to cover the excess on the policy.

Two of 'Edinburgh's Finest' eventually arrived to take a statement. They questioned both of them at length and implied they thought it was an inside job! It was – just not by them! Before leaving, one of the constables asked both how much money they had on their person.

David checked and had approx £150 and when asked, Chic admitted to having £1100. You couldn't make this up! David was gob-smacked.

"How much?"

"£1100," replied Chic.

Putting two and two together, they were handcuffed and huckled off to the city jail. It took four hours of negotiating to get them free.

My take on it was: David couldn't have been the brains of the operation – he only got £150 of the supposed ill-gotten gains, whilst the wee old cellar man got £1100, (didn't trust banks).

# Baby it's cold outside . . .

On one of my rare evenings off I had just poured a well-deserved drink when I caught sight of two policemen entering the bar. I had not been checking the CCTV as it was relatively quiet and there were more than enough staff on. Within a few minutes I was summoned by the head barmaid, Sarah.

On entering the bar I noticed a few of the local rugby team looking extremely dishevelled and somewhat sheepish. In fact, a couple seemed to be in a total state of undress i.e. naked! It appeared that they had disrobed on leaving another hostelry, streaked all the way down the High Street, passing the church and an old folks home, from whence the complaint had originated, (touch of jealousy methinks). They had arrived at our pub and merely joined the company of their friends as if this was an everyday occurrence, which for them it usually was.

This was not the view taken by the officers and although we were not responsible, the blame seemed to be being laid at our door. They were interrogating Sarah and implying that she was not in control of the bar; they were right. To be honest, she wasn't in control of herself, they were all big lads and you don't get many of them to the pound, especially on a quiet Sunday night.

After a lengthy lecture, off went the plods and the boys, totally unconcerned, didn't even bother to maintain their modesty. As one wit put it, what did it matter? Most of them were like a button on a fur coat anyway (work that out.)

NB. It is always the one who *shouldn't* strip off who does. There are only so many times you can blame the temperature!

# Time to say goodbye . . .

One of my most popular bar staff was a six foot hunk of gorgeous manhood called Zander. Every woman in the town was mad for him and he minced about the bar like a fairy on steroids. He was the most camp, cutting bitch I'd ever met and he could say the most outrageous things to guys as well as women and get away with it. Except for one small group of homophobic idiots.

Zander worked as a polo trainer. He handled huge beasts day in and day out and worked out with some of the toughest guys around. But he had a problem with this lot. Not so me!

One particular night I came into the bar and it was obvious he was upset; he was mincing up and down like an ostrich on speed. Saying nothing, just listening, I heard the ring leader shout.

"Pink gin, let's have a pink gin!"

I mean how original! Before Zander could do anything I stepped forward and took over the order.

"Four bottles of Bud, Linda."

"Fine, no problem," and he handed me a £20 note.

"That will be eighteen pounds!" I shouted back.

"Eighteen fucking quid! You're having a laugh!"

"Not at all," says I, spinning round with four extra glasses all containing pink gins.

"What the fuck?" He spluttered.

"Your order, sir."

Kept them quiet for a while . . .

Zander was extremely handsome and looked a bit like a blonde David Seaman, and he and I were the absolute best of pals. He'd come in during the day, into what he called 'God's waiting room'. He always maintained I couldn't give the punters credit as they were hardly likely to live long enough to pay it back.

On rare occasions he would drag up and become Zandra. Now Zandra was pure evil. This creation was an unadulterated, sheer bitch and the funniest person I have ever come across. Lily Savage was an absolute amateur in comparison. She would always pick on the most timid of men, (remember she was 6' 3" without the stilettos) and she terrorised them, but deep down Zander was desperately unhappy and although he camped it up and was always the life and soul of any party, he hated his life.

He had terrible night terrors and had taken to just appearing in my room at all times of the night. This didn't go down too well with my husband who would roar at him to "Fuck off home or I will give you terrors!"

Early in January the owner of the business next

door had terrible debts and it had been too much for him; he had committed suicide. I was shocked to the core and I made Zander promise me that no matter how bad he felt, he would never do such a thing. He gave me his word and also assured me he would never do that to his old mum.

Two weeks later his mother called me early one morning to check he was with me. The police found him later that day. He had gone to a local beauty spot and jumped from a bridge.

I have never been to, or seen, a funeral like his. If only he had realised how loved he was by everyone. I threw a huge party afterwards and it was amazing. People from every walk of life. All the Horsey Brigade and the Cunty Set (no, that's not a typo), rubbing shoulders with more drag queens than appeared in 'The Bird Cage,' plus all the closet gays from around the town, together with our regulars, even the 'Pink Gin Mob'.

Such a waste, he would have had the time of his life!

# Who's that lady???

Infidelity is rife in any bar or inn and we certainly had our fair share. We have had people climb out of toilet windows, shin down fire escapes and hide in the wheelie bins. In fact, if ever things get really bad I could always indulge in a little blackmail.

One memorable occasion, John and Alison, who were regulars and ate in the restaurant most Friday nights, were the cause of much hilarity and gossip. They arrived as usual about 6.30pm, had a couple of drinks, studied the menu and made their choices (nothing unusual in that).

They knew, and were known, to most of the staff and the regular Friday night customers. They made their way to their usual table and settled down to enjoy their meal.

Just as the waitress was about to clear the table, John began slowly sliding down his chair but Alison either didn't notice or just completely ignored the situation. The waitress cleared the table and headed off to the kitchen, bemused but none the wiser.

Approaching with the next course she realised

John had completely disappeared, presumably under the table, but his companion appeared oblivious to the situation. Unable to contain herself she asked the woman if she knew her husband had passed out and was under the table.

"No, he hasn't," came the reply, "he's just walked in the door."

# Watch the birdie . . .

We were once asked to cater for a large wedding to be held in the grounds of one of our local stately homes. It was a lavish affair and everything had gone perfectly.

We were at the coffee and speeches and really, as far as the catering service was concerned, there was nothing now that could go wrong. We could heave a huge sigh of relief. What happened next will go down in history.

I have never been so gobsmacked or flabbergasted in my life. Thank God it had nothing to do with us. As I said, it was a huge wedding and no expense had been spared. The speeches were underway and it was time for the groom to address the company.

He began by thanking everyone for attending and, of course, thanked his wife's parents for the magnificent party, saying as a token of his appreciation he had a personal gift for each of them.

Under each chair he had taped an envelope. He asked everyone to open their envelopes. Most guests were expecting a lottery or raffle ticket, but none expected the contents they got. A full colour photograph of the bride and the best man indulging in some pre-marital hanky panky.

The groom chose that moment to leave.

Honestly, this actually happened.

# Chefs . . .

I could write a book on this subject alone.

I have had in my time, two murderers, one embezzler, one bigamist (with three girlfriends as well), countless drug dealers, and even countless more drug takers; four alcoholics (serious alcoholics) one suffering from Multiple Personality Disorder, shame only one of the personalities could cook; more thieves than Ali Baba, and a sprinkling of fabulous ones. They, however, usually proved to be extremely boring and not worth writing about.

Let's take the case of Robert. He arrived on the scene via an agency; that in itself should have warned me. Good chefs have permanent jobs. But once again, I was desperate. He arrived at about eight o'clock one Sunday evening and I was appalled at his appearance. I almost stopped him from entering the building, he was so dishevelled and unkempt, virtually a down-and-out. But it was Sunday in the country, no buses. I would deal with him in the morning.

Arriving in the kitchen, a little after 7am just in case, I was met by this immaculate chef, in pristine whites, hat and scarf; (most of the other kitchen inhabitants rolled up in whatever they had been wearing the night before or even the night before that). His gleaming utensils were laid out on his work bench and he had obviously been at work for some time. It turned out he had been waiting on the doorstep for the cleaning staff to arrive. I was astounded and kept looking around for the troll from the night before to suddenly jump out at me. What a transformation.

I thought all my Christmases and birthdays had come at once. He was absolutely fantastic and had worked in every top establishment in the country. Always a bit vague as to why he was not still in any of these temples, but I was so blessed to have him I didn't push the subject. He took the kitchen in hand and within a couple of weeks had transformed things.

He decided to change the menu and came up with the most amazing dishes. Then the proverbial hit the fan. Four weeks into his stay and I had already told the agency we were hoping to keep him on. I found their reaction somewhat reticent and they urged us to give it a bit longer. I was soon to learn why.

Robert had gone off home on Sunday evening as usual, for his two days off. He'd left strict instructions to run all the kitchen stocks down and get in the supplies for the new menu to begin on his return. He intended to train everyone up on Wednesday to cope with the weekend onslaught.

It was with great anticipation we all looked

forward to his return on Wednesday. As a rule he was exactingly prompt and when he had not arrived by 10.30am I began to worry and dread something had happened to him. At around 11am he phoned to say his car had broken down and he would be late.

One thing you have in the licensed trade is contacts, and I had several in the AA and RAC. I had patrol cars rushing between Perth and Glasgow, and Glasgow and Edinburgh, looking for this poor stranded chef.

Then the penny dropped.

Fuck! He didn't drive. He'd lost his licence years previously. I phoned his mobile again and again, and eventually called the agency. It was obvious from their reaction that this was not unusual for Robert. In fact, he had lasted longer than usual with us.

Robert and his wife were serious alcoholics. He would binge-drink for a couple of weeks, dry out for a week and then go back to work. This was a monthly occurrence. Everyone in the trade knew, except me. Now not only was I faced with no chef, I had no one who could work the bloody menu he had devised.

It was obviously his modus operandi as no sooner had I told the agency that I would be suing them, they miraculously came up with a chef who could implement the menu. It seemed that 'poor Robert' had done this on more than one occasion, and, unlike me, the agency had a backup plan.

We got through the first couple of weeks with

'Desperate Dan the Rescue Man' but he had none of 'poor Robert's' flair or imagination, none of his drinking habits either. He really was a watered-down version of the genius that was Rab.

Perhaps because of that, and because I am a mug with a capital M, when Robert surfaced, he pleaded and begged to be allowed back. He knew I was his last chance. Reluctantly I agreed, on the strict condition he would attend AA. I later found out the nearest he got to that was my mobilizing the breakdown service; wrong type of breakdown.

We got eight weeks out of him which was okay. It took us through the busy summer period. Then the wagon lost a wheel and off he tumbled. He actually went in the middle of service and because of this, I thought something had happened other than booze. He just disappeared in the middle of plating up an order. One minute he was there, the next, gone. We searched the building from top to bottom to no avail. The demons had him again.

Every one in the village knew Rab was off chasing spooks and a couple of weeks after his vanishing act, two kids from the next village came to the kitchen door to tell us they knew where our chef was.

He had been sleeping rough in a burned-out car on the Earl of Wemyss' estate. No cardboard box under a viaduct for him. Not once during his MIA had his wife called to enquire why her husband had not arrived home. I was later to discover why.

Well, we got him back and to the best of our ability sorted him out. That was when I came up with my plan; there was no doubt the man was a genius but he was as reliable as British Rail.

His drinking followed a pattern and it was fairly easy to work out what to do. No way could he continue as head chef and by now two of my other chefs had improved under his tutelage, beyond all expectations.

So we had Robert on a week to week basis. Everyone was instructed to watch him like a hawk and this actually worked for about six months. Until one night he just disappeared into the evening mist and I never saw him alive again. He and his wife had indulged in one too many drinking sessions and Robert actually died in his sleep.

He lay undiscovered for three days, despite the fact that Mrs. Robert was in the same room.

# More chefs . . .

As I've said, chefs are a motley crew. Just look at Gordon Ramsay: his behaviour is anything but normal and I have to say, if he'd ever worked alongside any of my guys, he would have a few more battle scars.

Maybe it's the heat, or the extreme pressure they work under but even the most normal have some foible or other. Most are heavy drinkers and at best, binge-drinkers.

I was so fed up with the buggers not turning up for work on a Sunday morning that I stopped paying them until end of shift on a Sunday, and if they wanted an advance on their wages for a couple of beers on a Saturday, the maximum was £20. None of them could get drunk on £20.

Gamblers are the best workers when they are losing, and they lose most of the time. They completely spend up on their day off and have no money for the rest of their free time, no hangovers and usually want as much overtime as possible. The downside of this is that if they do have the occasional win, they are off and running and you don't see them for days.

# The Hitman and . . .

For a while my head chef and second chef were a double act from Glasgow who wreaked havoc across the county for months. The head chef, William, was an excellent cook and could work under pressure like no other chef I've ever come across. We were a terrifically busy restaurant but he was a serious menace, of the worst kind. A street fighter who was always bragging about his 'connections'.

He was the second cousin, twice removed, of someone involved in the 'Glasgow Ice-Cream Wars'. Personally I think he bought a 99 cone from one of their vans and that was his only claim to fame.

He had been an amateur boxer in his youth and had been destined for great things. But no one had told him that drink, drugs and women do not Olympic gold medals make. He, like many before him, had missed the boat and he had become just a surly thug with an enormous chip on his shoulder.

After work he would strut about the bar like an ugly little bantam cock. I forgot to mention how ugly he was, and yet women swarmed round him. He was a seriously bad drunk and was always on the lookout for his next victim. His sidekick James was a reasonable enough chef; nothing special but they worked well together, in and out of the kitchen.

They always played the 'I've got you over a barrel' game with me, and would frequently make jokes about how if they left, the kitchen would close and we couldn't dispense with their services. And many other such enlightening quips.

The downfall for this pair was that they never gave anyone else credit for being able to add two plus two. Actually, I wasn't sure if they could master such advanced maths. It was time to divide and separate.

William had decided he was having an extra holiday between Christmas and New Year. It probably would have been fine, if only he had run it past me. But such was his ego he was convinced on his return he would spin 'the stupid cow' (me) a line, and all would be well. However, this stupid cow had been planting a few seeds and had managed to get chef number two on my side. He was furious that William had taken off and had left him with the brunt of the work with not even a by your leave.

That particular week is manic and no one gets time off. So to help ease the pressure, I pandered to James' ego and gave him and the remaining chefs an extra bonus. I also started the rumour that William had been given the Christmas bonus to divide amongst them and it looked like he had buggered off and spent it. He hadn't, but who would they believe? All this, to ensure that when he did show up he would have no backup. He was going, but not taking the whole brigade with him.

On the 3rd or 4th of January, he strolled into the bar, having first made sure I had left for the night, and proceeded to hold court; telling of his adventures. His story was that he had been abducted by a 'Glasgow hit mob' and driven, blindfold, somewhere down south. Apparently he owed them a favour and it had been called in. According to him you certainly didn't argue with those guys.

As the story unfolded, we learned that he had been given a gun and instructions (not sure if these were about the firing mechanism, but presumably about his victims). It was three days before they had returned and he was able to carry out his contract.

There actually *had* been a terrible incident in London at the time and police really were appealing for witnesses, and here we had the perpetrator sitting in the bar telling all and sundry that he had done it, and how. Now I don't think I've come across many hit men in my time, but even if I had, I wouldn't expect them to advertise their occupation.

There were at least a dozen witnesses to his confession and we also had it taped on CCTV. Given that he was known to the police, it was hardly surprising that a few well-meaning citizens who had suffered at this buffoon's hands, reported to the boys in blue that the culprit was in East Lothian.

The staff cottage was raided the next morning and it was reported on the lunchtime news that a man was 'assisting them with their enquiries'.   He obviously had nothing to do with the crime, but he had two outstanding warrants for unpaid fines and an overdue library book.  That was the last we saw of him.

James stayed with us for a few weeks but without his protector, took a quite few second prizes in encounters with the locals and he soon moved on to pastures new.

# The Cider Man . . .

I always find it fascinating how differently people appear to others. Take the Cider Man for example. He was to us, an extremely well dressed, well groomed chap who came into the bar most nights. He always stood alone, never had any inclination to join in bar room banter and steadfastly ignored any suggestion he might want to enter into conversation, with either customer or barmaid.

He had two pints of super strength cider and left. This ritual continued for several years and it was only when I took over another establishment that I saw another side to him.

Not once in all the years he had visited the Tweedy, did I suspect that the cider he consumed with us was not his only drink of the evening. It turned out, that we were only one of four or five hostelries he visited nightly, on his way home from work. His last port of call was our new home and he arrived at about 8pm each evening.

Previously we had regarded him as well groomed: not by the time he'd finished his rounds. Once thought of as quiet and stand-offish, here we couldn't shut him up. After probably eight pints of Dynamite he was certainly the life and soul of the party. I often wondered what his wife and family must have felt about his behaviour as this was a nightly occurrence.

He was a real high flyer in local government, lived in a lovely house and had all the trappings of a decent 'executive life' but eventually the wife left, taking their daughter. He lost his job and became more and more shabby. The last I heard of him he was doing agency work and the house was on the market.

But he still maintained the façade that he only had two pints of cider.

# The Three Marys . . .

Believe it or not, Big Mary and Wee Mary were sisters. Who said that parents had no imagination? Actually, they were stepsisters and were never apart. When you saw one, the other was only a mere footstep away. I quickly figured out this wasn't because they adored one another, quite the opposite in fact; more to make sure that the other sister didn't get one iota, or crumb of anything more than the other.

They had been thrown together fairly young; the product of a second marriage, and from day one had competed for everything. The last biscuit, who had the bigger boiled egg, you've had one drink more than me. It was even rumoured that they had two 52" flat-screen TV's in their sitting room so they could watch different channels at the same time. They say that truth is stranger than fiction and how strange is this? They were born on the same day; it was three years apart, but still?

Big Mary was 5'2", not exactly Amazonian, and Wee Mary was 5' so if the big one was wearing trainers and the little one was wearing heels, Big Mary was actually Little Mary and Little Mary became Big Mary. Confused? You will be. They didn't dress exactly alike but as near as damn it. They usually managed to colour coordinate and were often mistaken for twins. They didn't really look alike but the whole persona gave that impression. It was difficult to pinpoint their ages but they looked to be in their late 30's or early 40's although that really is guesswork.

The parents had long departed this mortal coil and had left the house and all that went with it to 'the girls'. Now, one wanted to sell up and move away but the other didn't, so there was a constant battle over 'the hoose'. At one time, I think it was Wee Mary who rented her half out to four Polish workers in an effort to force the situation. But Big Mary was having none of it. She was in situ, so she, having increased the rent already agreed with Wee Mary, collected it. Wee Mary was out of pocket and out of the house, so that didn't last long.

I am sure they would have continued this strange existence ad infinitum until George Clooney entered the picture. Actually it was a fifty year old, ex-priest called Michael, aka 'My Boyfriend'. It is difficult to imagine that this insignificant weedy-looking chap could engender such passion in two such confirmed spinsters. But he did.

The competition was in deadly earnest now and it was *the* most absurd ménage a trois. They seemed to have worked out a kind of rota system which didn't work because they were both regulars in the same bar. So when Michael was out with Big Mary, Little Mary would just join them and pay for her own drinks, and when Little Mary was the significant other, then Big Mary would do the same. To everyone but the threesome it was hysterical.

This situation went on for almost a year with Michael getting thinner and thinner and paler and paler and looking as if he was at death's door. I should imagine servicing that pair, in all ways, would exhaust anyone and he wasn't the most sturdy of chaps to begin with.

Now, at this stage we've not met 'Anybody's Mary' or AM as she was affectionately known. I am sure you don't need an explanation regarding her nickname. AM was 'Big Mary' and 'Little Mary's' cousin and she was some gal. She had been married and divorced at least three times and had a string of paramours the length and breadth of the country.

She had gone off to Turkey for a week's holiday with another of her benevolent pals the previous year, and as was her wont, met someone and stayed. It would seem this romance had run its course and here she was back. As big and as bold as ever.

AM was as different to her two cousins as chalk and cheese. Within hours of being back she had charmed everyone with her raucous tales and sexy banter and was already dancing on the tables; a blatant exhibitionist. The cousins were appalled and clinging on to 'My Boyfriend' for dear life. Michael, on the other hand, was mesmerised.

'Anybody's Mary' had arrived, bag and baggage, and expected the cousins to accommodate her as they always had. It was the one thing about which they were united, their love and envy of their feckless cousin. But things were different now. They knew if they let her under their roof, 'My Boyfriend' would be a thing of the past but what could they do?

It took ten days, just ten days. They came home from work to find a note saying: 'Thanks, we'll call you when we get settled.'

*We'll?* Who was the other half of *We'll?* Of course it was the George Clooney look-alike, aka 'My Boyfriend.' The pair had gone off to Benidorm to run a bar owned by one of AM'S ex's. And by all accounts they are still there, blissfully happy.

Big Mary and Wee Mary? They still hate each other but they hate her more!

# The One Armed Bandit . . .

Every pub has at least one one-armed bandit, aka the fruit machine or 'the puggy' but here in the Tweedy we had the real thing. We actually had a 'one armed bandit' called Sean. Now Sean was an idiot, the fact that he only had one arm is testament to that. He was born with both but managed to lose one somewhere along the line. There were so many tales as to how that happened; from a shark bite to a paper cut that went septic, we'll just agree he managed to lose one.

Prior to his loss, I believe he was a fairly successful bank robber. Successful in that he had avoided capture and lived a fairly good life. Things had changed. Oh, he still aspired to be a bank robber but when you have to ask your captors to open the door for your getaway, it loses some of its threat.

Never one to be defeated, Sean came up with more solutions to his problem than tongue can tell. On occasions when he was just short of money he would pull a pair of tights over his face, walk into a building society or bank and demand money.

I never knew why the disguise. I always felt the

one arm was a dead giveaway. Imagine how long it would take to form an Identity Parade? I mean, how many forty year olds are there in any town with just one arm? So he got caught time and time again. Fortunately for him, the judges all seemed to take pity on him and he had so many hours of community service backed up, it would take him till the other arm dropped off to complete them.

He decided he was going for one last big one. One that would set him up in the Costa del Crime, living the life of Riley. He had a number of prostheses (artificial limbs) which he hated, but they might just do the trick.

Solution number one was to fix the gun onto the artificial hand and bend it into position, which he did. Off he went to secure his future. Right in the middle of the raid, the weight of the gun toppled the limb. It fell off, the cashier fainted and again he had to ask for help to get out. Not a success.

Solution number two was much the same as solution number one but involved more gaffer tape, super glue and blue tack!

Back into town and to a bank he had not tried to raid before, which was becoming rarer and rarer. Barging through the swing doors, screaming at the customers to get down on the floor and generally sounding like a real robber.

This time it wasn't the arm that was the main problem. He was wearing thicker tights than normal and was having a bit of trouble negotiating his way round the floor without stepping on the stricken customers. Unfortunately, he bumped into a heavy metal waste bin which set off the gun. He shot himself in the foot and hopped screaming, out into the arms of the local constabulary.

Unfortunately, on this occasion there was a woman judge on the bench, who had little or no time for the Seans of this world, and off he went for an extended holiday, just not in the sun.

# Back from the dead . . .

I have never believed in coincidence. I believe things happen for a reason, maybe not the reason you hoped for, but a reason all the same.

For years I had Thursday afternoon and evening as my time off, usually just to set me up for the start of the weekend, so this occasion was very unusual; in fact, I think this was the only time I ever worked the tea-time shift.

The story began in the early 60's when a local lad went missing. The two theories concerning his disappearance were that he had fallen in the River Esk and had been carried out to sea, or he had been taken by gypsies who were camping in the area. Whatever the reason; poor Craig was never seen again. I can still remember seeing his distraught mother walking by the river, wailing and grief stricken. Living in such close proximity was too much for her so the family convinced her to move to another part of the town.

Craig was never forgotten and there had been countless sightings of him over the years, but all proved fruitless. They were a loving and caring family and they pulled together through this time.

As I said, the chances of me being in the bar on that particular day, was a real long shot. Had it been any other member of staff, what happened next would mean nothing to them.

There were only a few stalwarts round the bar watching 'Deal or No Deal' or some other intellectual programme. A lad came in who I had not seen before, and ordered a drink. As I'm pouring him his drink he babbles on about having been to the Job Centre and how inefficient they are and quite honestly, I probably switched off and just nodded in the right places. However, something he said switched my attention back on. He was asking about members of his family. He was trying to contact them but they had moved and he mentioned the name, Moran.

Now as I said, had anyone else been serving, it's unlikely the name would have meant anything. I started probing the guy about who he was looking for. He began to get quite agitated and suddenly came out with accusations about the family and how they had been awful to him. That's why it had taken thirty years for him to come back. He insinuated he had been the victim of child abuse and hadn't I guessed now who he was?

All this information and conversation took about ten minutes and was pretty off-the-wall. If someone had been missing for all these years and carefully kept their real identity secret, it didn't ring true that ten minutes in a bar would make them spill out all this information to a total stranger. He boldly stated he knew things that no one outside the family would know and that was the proof of who he was. I was absolutely appalled and I couldn't believe anyone would put their family through the trauma that he had. I didn't for a minute believe his allegations and told him so. At which point he left the bar.

Of course, this was a fantastic diversion to those sitting round the bar and who the hell cares how much is in a fucking red box, this was much better.

Now I was in a quandary as to what to do. I couldn't ignore it, if on the very slightest chance this person was who he claimed to be. I decided to phone the daughter-in-law, who I knew fairly well. I certainly didn't want the old couple to be upset. However, one clever bugger thought it would be in everyone's interest to call the local papers. Well, you can imagine what happened next. It was blown into a huge story and of course the Morans had their hopes raised yet again.

While all this was going on I maintained he was a fraud, as did the police. Hearing about his problems at the Job Centre they organised a stake-out, reasoning that he must attend there at a specific time and maybe they would catch him the following week.

Meanwhile, CCTV shots were examined and two possible suspects were identified. Remember, I don't believe in coincidence. My husband and a customer were in the rec room in the police station, going through the CCTV when a visiting PC came in for a coffee. Spying the shot of our man on the television, he asked.

"What's he done now?"

"You know this guy?"

"Of course I do, he's an idiot from town called Moran, can't remember his first name."

It was the lad's cousin and yes, he probably did know things that the general public would not have been aware of, but to do this to your own family?

What happened to him? Frankly, bugger all, but the damage he did was immeasurable.

I have not seen or heard of this person for approximately ten years. Yet within two hours of writing this he was standing before me in a queue buying a bottle of milk and a bottle of vodka. How's that for a coincidence?

# Wedding favour!!!

Staff weddings always cost us a fortune if the wedding is on the premises. The member of staff wants everything for nothing. After all, "I work here." One incident made me so bitter I almost banned weddings all together, (staff ones that is.) Mind you after thirty nine years of wedded bliss maybe I should enforce that rule!

One of my staff whom I thought to be a really lovely girl, Tracy, had worked for me for over four years and we had done her engagement party, her son's christening and now came the big day. I have to say I did expect it to be in another venue, but no, she wanted it to be with us. Being the mug that I was, I allowed her free rein. She spent months planning the day and spared no cost (or rather, *I* didn't).

We had recently hired a new manageress (Fiona) who was a real livewire. She wasn't as popular with the staff as perhaps she expected to be, but hey ho! She was there to do a job and make sure everything ran like clockwork. Tracy and Fiona could be seen closeted at every opportunity, ironing out the fine details. Eventually the Big Day arrived. It was a wonderful occasion for the happy couple, their respective families and all our staff. Nothing was left to chance and it was as near perfect as possible.

The cost of her wedding for a hundred guests, including food, the toast, flowers and of course, service, should have been £7,000. My gift to them was that she paid only the cost price, £4,000 and her friends and colleagues worked for nothing; that was their gift.

Off they went on their honeymoon, which we had managed to get a fabulous deal on, through one of our customers. Short of marrying the bloke myself there was bugger all else I could have done for them.

Then came the bombshell. I received a text from the Seychelles to say she had hated working for me, and since Fiona had arrived it was even worse. She couldn't face coming back. She was so very disappointed that no one thought enough of them to merit a wedding gift and because of these two issues she would not be back. Shame she hadn't worked that out the week before her wedding. I would have charged her the full amount and bought her a toaster from Comet.

Most of the staff were as gobsmacked as I was but it emerged from the ones who were close to her that she had planned this all along. She had decided to leave months earlier, but wanted to have her wedding at cost price. Well she was due it, wasn't she?

I am happy to say that three years down the line they have separated. I wonder where she'll hold her divorce party?

# And another . . .

I seem to be the kiss of death to weddings. You'd think I would learn. Another of our girls had the wedding from hell but this time it was someone else's responsibility.

Janie was man mad. She had new boyfriends, week in, week out and everything was always so intense. Despite warnings from everyone she embarked on another great 'Love Story.'

Every two years the Welsh invade Scotland for the rugby and every town around Edinburgh is alive with the bhoyos. Every pub resounds to male voice choirs and, win or lose, it is a great time. Now, Janie was out with some girls and on the prowl. Like in the song 'Across a Crowded Room'– can you hear the music? She spotted Shane. He must have been standing on the table at the time as he is the smallest Welshman I've ever seen. But, he was a charmer. This boy from the valleys could charm the knickers off a nun. Well, it was love, and they spent every remaining moment together; he even missed the match and, on the Sunday evening before he left, he proposed.

Everyone expected this great love affair to fizzle out, but no, they hadn't reckoned on Janie's tenacity. She had exhausted the supply of local lads and was now having to work further afield.

They met and were engaged in February; by the end of April, she was pregnant and the wedding was on and scheduled for July. I declined the offer to 'do it', pleading another booking. I have to say I wasn't too involved with the planning but she and her mother certainly pulled everything out of the hat and another 'Big Day' duly arrived.

I didn't get to the reception till mid evening, but to all intents and purposes, the wedding had gone well, until Shane, who'd had more than a few beers, got in tow with a group of Janie's ex's. It must have come as quite a shock to find out she wasn't the blushing virgin he had thought, and that the paternity of her last child was so in question there had been a book run on it. They welcomed Shane with open arms; after all he was taking the pressure off them!

As the party drew to a close, the bridegroom was more than a few sheets to the wind and the final straw was seeing his new bride in the clutches of one of her ex's, mooning around the dance floor. Enough was enough. Shane grabbed the mike and called the company to attention. He announced to all and sundry that he had made a terrible mistake, probably the biggest mistake of his life. At that point the bride's mother jumped to her daughter's defence.

The mother-in-law from hell dropkicked the groom and threw him over the bannister. No real damage done, they were only one flight up. Then it was Wales versus Scotland in earnest; I have to say the Scots won the scrum easily.

Shane wandered off into the night with the bridesmaid, Stacy, in tow. It seemed they spent the night in the bridal suite which had been *my* wedding present to the happy couple. In future, the only wedding gifts were definitely going to be toasters from Comet, with the receipt attached.

Shane eventually returned to Wales with his new wife but it turned out to be another marriage that didn't last the pace. Within one year they had met, conceived, married, given birth, and split up.

Eventful, to say the least. A record, even for us!

# Boo!!!

Every pub, so they say, has at least one ghost and we were no exception. But ours was one of the more peculiar ones. I just don't think it knew it was a ghost! Firstly its abode was odd. It hung about in the pool room, or in the corridor next door.

I first became aware of her a few weeks after we moved in. She was always very evident just as we were about to lock up. I have already explained how we had to check the gents toilets. Well, the pool room was next to them. This room had no windows; it was adjacent to the hall next door, running the length of the building. It had a very heavy door which we always kept wedged open. This was for security purposes, mainly to stop any drug trafficking or any other naughty goings on.

However, no matter what time of night we finished and went to lock up, the door was closed. This happened every night and just as the door was wedged open again, you would catch a glimpse of someone just out the corner of your eye. This was never spooky, just curious and always took me by surprise. I didn't mention this to anyone for some time, mainly because they thought I was a bit mad, and this would reinforce that belief.

One night I was chatting with Alan, the chap next door and he jokingly said we must have upset Esther the ghost, because lately in the morning when they opened up, she had been on the rampage and things were scattered along the passageway. This was the passage which ran the full length of our building. If she walked through the wall, she would be standing in my pool room. The building next door had at one time been a cinema and legend had it, she was an usherette who had never clocked off.

Now I neither believe, nor disbelieve, in ghosts. I can only tell you what happened. Around about closing time, as I said, the door would mysteriously close and there would be the most overpowering smell of Jeyes Fluid – yes – Jeyes Fluid. Nothing else; just a closed door and the smell. We obviously weren't as interesting as the carpet shop next door. That was, until the refurbishment.

Six months after we moved in, the brewery agreed to do a major refurbishment which would mean closing for approximately six weeks and amongst the changes, the pool room was about to become our kitchen. Esther was going to be upset.

During the construction of the kitchen the men on site were spooked constantly, with things going missing and turning up in the oddest of places. Lights went on and off and lots of other strange things happened. Alan next door, however, had little or no activity. I think for once, we were more interesting.

The refurbishment was complete and we now boasted a fabulous new kitchen, complete with dry goods cupboard. Coincidentally, this cupboard had been built just where we had almost caught sight of her in the past. She was in her element. Lots of things to move and examine – and she did.

At first the girls were a bit scared and it was rather spooky, but they soon got used to it and would yell.

"Esther get me some flour!" Or sugar or whatever.

When they were busy, and I promise you this is no lie, on more than one occasion whatever had been asked for would appear. There was one recurring incident, however, that defied explanation.

There were three shelves running round the inside of the cupboard and the bottom and top were very spacious, but the middle was not. All our flour products were kept in large containers, which fitted easily into two of the shelves but were almost impossible to fit in the middle. Guess what we had to do almost every morning before beginning work? Yes, we had to prise all these containers off the middle shelf. This also happened frequently during service which was infuriating as we had no time to bugger about.

Now I know most ghosts walk around with their heads tucked under their arm, and others rattle chains; ours seemed to be content moving boxes of fish batter from shelf to shelf; not very interesting? Well when it's your fish batter it is!

You may well be right, maybe someone got up every morning and battered these bins into place, maybe someone was playing tricks on us, but I know what I know and I was sad to leave her when we moved on.

# Is there anybody there ? ? ?

The Inn was an old blacksmith's forge with four workers cottages linked together. They had been built in the late 1700's for migrant workers (yes, they had them back then). Conditions would have been difficult and there must have been countless deaths over the years. It is not surprising that sightings of ghosts and spectres were numerous. As I said I neither believe nor disbelieve, I can only repeat what others have reported.

Unlike friendly Esther in Tweedy's, the inhabitants of The County were far more threatening and frightening, and different ghosts haunted different parts of the building. Maybe they had territorial boundaries. I wonder what happened if one crossed into another; they could hardly murder each other!

So we have established that these ghosts were not the Caspar type figures. There was a Grey Lady (there's always a Grey Lady). A little girl who was always crying, (now there's a change), and assorted wailers, grinders and gnashers of teeth. However, the man who spent his time in the function room, formerly the old forge, was definitely the most frightening and the one spoken about the most.

It was said to be the local blacksmith and during the lead up to the Battle of Preston Pans he had been commandeered by the English army, led by Sir John Cope, to provide weapons for his army. Being a loyal Scot, he resisted all attempts to make him work and eventually he was murdered by two English soldiers, who held him down in the cooling trough. Now whether that story bears any resemblance to the truth, I cannot tell.

Several staff had experienced a feeling of being crowded or oppressed. They would suddenly feel a presence closing in on them and then feel as though something was leaning heavily on them. This was experienced by lots of staff and also by a customer. Normally I would put it down to alcohol, but this customer was a 'designated driver' and she had been drinking soft drinks all evening.

Having forgotten her mobile phone, she had gone back to collect it. Alone in the function suite and leaning over the table, she thought a member of staff had come in. Turning to speak there was no one there. She then had the sensation that someone, or something, was trying to hold her down, and she actually had a slight burn on her forehead from candles which had still been alight on the table. She was extremely frightened and it took some time to calm her down.

Due to the number of sightings throughout the

building and also because it was good publicity, we arranged to have an exorcism or 'cleansing' carried out. Now I don't know what I expected, but there certainly was no one 'pinned to the ceiling' nor 'heads round the wrong way'. The television was still showing the footie and there was no mention of 'Caroline stepping away from the white light'.

A fairly ordinary looking gentleman walked through the building swinging some sort of incense burner and muttering. He got to the back door, held out his hand for the money and left! Well I can tell you – was I bloody mad? I thought I had been well and truly cleansed, cleansed of a hundred quid! I marched up to the forge and dared that fucking ghost to reappear.

Strangely enough his presence has never been felt since. Maybe the cleansing did work, or maybe it was me!

# K. P . . . Nuts!

Over the years I have had countless kitchen porters (K.P.s) and they have usually had one thing in common, apart from drink; they are thick. C'mon, you'd have to be, to work in those conditions for half the pay everyone else gets. But one shines out above all the others.

Andy worked for us for probably ten years. He had been a Master Baker (try saying that quickly) but developed an allergy to flour. Personally I think he developed an allergy to the hours, as they interfered with his drinking. Whatever the reason, he came to join our happy little band. Another misfit in the mix.

Now that I remember, he came to fill in for his wife, who had a major hangover, certainly worse than his, and she was on a final, final warning. I think he just stayed and she went off somewhere else to work.

He could have single-handedly kept an ambulance-chasing lawyer in silk ties for a year. He was the most accident-prone person I have ever met. During a routine environmental health visit, the officer asked to see our accident book. She nearly had a fit and accused us of making it up. It took some convincing we had not. She advised me to sack him as he was a liability. Well, I would have had no kitchen staff left if they were sacked on that count!

On a typical day, he put a 12lb turkey back into the freezer and it promptly fell out and knocked him out. Christ, the egg on his forehead looked like it had been laid by the turkey. He skidded and slipped around the kitchen like Bambi on ice and would grab anyone and anything to steady himself. It was not advisable to let him near knives, but sometimes you had to. So at frequent times throughout the day you would hear the plaintive cry.

"Where's the plasters? I'm bleeding again."

Any other member of staff having a mishap and requiring plasters were invariably out of luck. He once had so many about his person he looked like a giant Smurf (kitchen plasters are blue).

He tried to stop smoking and bought a month's supply of patches. They didn't work because:

a) he was immune to the patch theory, he had been wearing so many for so long and

b) he usually had them round a cut or bruise somewhere else on his body.

Like most kitchens, on busy days you invariably run out of supplies and the K.P. is the gopher. With Andy you had to be precise to the point of ridicule. One Saturday we had had a real run on large Yorkshire puddings stuffed with roast beef and gravy. To complete the orders, I hurriedly sent Andy off to get more supplies. He was away for some time and I was getting concerned. Back he came carrying a large Woolworth's bag which he emptied onto my work station. Out fell a dozen family size bars of Cadbury's Fruit and Nut; we stood open mouthed at his purchases.

"I'm sorry" he said "I couldn't get giant Yorkies!"

# Quizzical . . .

The average pub quiz is a bit of fun on a dreary winter's evening which no one takes very seriously and is an excuse to get away from the wife and kids. That is except for the 'Quizzers'.

These are teams of intellectuals who never miss a match and are normally sourced from the Social Work Department or the local primary school. Their teams have Latin names that not even they can pronounce, and they consume half a lager and a packet of crisps between them, that is until they win first prize when it's brandy and coke all round. So intent are they on their quizzing, that if a particular pub caters for the hoi poloi, they will not deign to enter.

So, most of our quizzes were beneath their contempt which suited us fine. My punters had very few brain cells between them. Some of them even thought a GCSE was a make of washing machine, and by the second half were usually too pissed to write. They had team names like 'The Dog's Bollocks' and 'All Fannies are Round'. Referring, of course, to that well known malapropism by Johnnie Craddock.

But we did cross paths; you see we were in the League. How we ever qualified I will never know. Maybe the last incumbent slept with someone of importance. Perhaps money had changed hands. Or maybe, they just needed to make up the numbers. Whatever the reason, we were in the League and there were inter-pub quizzes into which we were obliged to enter a team. These quizzes were held monthly in a variety of establishments and they were catered.

Now we were definitely fourth division in the quiz tables, but when it came to the catering we were absolutely top of the Premier League and thus the only reason 'The Nil Desperandum's' and the 'Quo Quid Pro's' would grace us with their presence. I never had a problem putting a team together on a monthly basis. In fact, it was a harder job keeping most of them out.

Then, of course, there were the groupies. Each team had its supporters, most of whom were very well behaved and so excited at the prospect of maybe taking part that they spent most of the time running back and fro to the toilets. Not so with my motley crew; oh they were excited all right, and yes they spent the time doing the toilet run, but for different reasons.

They would roar the answer to their team-mates; the fact that it was usually wrong proved no deterrent. As for support, by closing time every one of them needed support. The fuckers could never stand. We were frowned upon! Now I take shit from no one and I certainly wasn't taking it from a load of camel-toed, sandal-wearing hippies who thought they were better than us. The fact they were had nothing to do with it. I had decided the next match held at home, my team would win. But how?

Honestly, I couldn't get anyone with as much as an 'O' level for love nor money. I tried importing from other pubs. No one would come, not even on the promise of a fabulous running buffet. I was getting desperate. Then I came up with 'The Plan': Google; I was going to Google and I came up with a devilish plot to avoid suspicion.

For two days before the quiz I had a run-through with my team and cohorts and it went swimmingly. Basically I had a five man team who would take part and I had a five man team who would cheat. Sound okay?

This is how it would work. Simplicity itself. What would happen was; each cheat was numbered and they would come through, ask the question, go into the toilet and by the time they returned I would have the answer which they would then pass to the team. We ran through the plan time and time again and had it working to perfection.

The catering was par excellence, the bar was warm and inviting and I had a winning team. The evening started absolutely to plan. The system was working. A cheat would come past me in the kitchen, go into either the gents or ladies, do a swift turn around, come past me, get the answer and pass it on as directed.

Round one full points, round two full points, round three full points, then things began to go wrong.

What had I not counted on? The cheating bastards were getting pissed! Cheat number one rolled into the toilet, met his mate and stood blethering with him about the job they'd just finished, missed his cue.

Cheat number two got cheat number one's answer. Then number three came in, joined in number one's chat; he missed his cue and got number four's answer. And to top it all cheat number five (Sharon) took so long doing her hair she missed a whole bloody category. What a fucking shambles. Round four, only one point.

Now I had to re-group them without drawing attention to the situation. Round five was general knowledge and we had to get back on track. We were in second place to 'Habeas Corpus' from the pub across the road; a bunch of toffee-nosed sods. I couldn't wait to wipe the smug smile off their faces. This was the last round and I was primed and ready to go.

Cheat number one came past pissed and I couldn't make out what the question was. So I dashed into the gents to find out what he'd said. Oh my God! Half the male population of the bar were in there.

By now cheat number two had passed by my stance and shouted the question into thin air. Now I had numbers one and two to answer and three was looming. I went as quick as Google could. Got the answers, shouted them so loudly that everyone in the bar who didn't know, now did. Suspicions were being raised.

Cheat number four and team member number five got into an argument about what question was he answering. I was under so much pressure I roared "Australia!" to the team captain of 'The Winner Takes All' who had just come to get some tomato sauce. The game was up. The plan had failed and we were disqualified.

"Fuck it," I thought.

If we weren't the winners, they were not getting the finger buffet. So with great aplomb, I removed all the remaining food and called a halt to the proceedings.

I have to say had it been anyone else but these nerds, I would have expected a riot, but, they stamped their feet, slammed their reference books and slunk off into the night.

At a league meeting we were barred for life. Who cared? Our quizzes were much better fun anyway!

# PUB QUIZ

## Food & Drink

1. What sort of pastry is used to make profiteroles?

2. What is the national dish of Hungary?

3. Which nut is used to flavour traditional Bakewell Tart?

4. From which country does Rioja wine come?

5. In the dish Beef Wellington, in what is the beef wrapped?

6. What is the main vegetable used to make Borsch?

7. From which part of Ireland does Murphy's stout originate?

8. What is Bombay Duck?

*Answers on page 214*

# Geography

1. In which European country is the city of Salzburg?

2. To which EU member state do the islands of Gozo and Comino belong?

3. Where in Italy can the Ponte Vecchio be found?

4. Into which sea does the River Danube flow?

5. Above which city does Panorama rise?

6. Known in Flemish as "Luik" what is the French name for this Belgian city?

7. Which European country is denoted by the letters 'CH' on motor vehicles?

8. Which European country was re-unified on 3rd October 1990?

*Answers on page 214*

# Music

1. Which singer fronted the pop band Duran Duran?

2. Which pop group had 1960s hits with songs written by Brian Wilson?

3. From which part of Britain does the pop band Stereophonics hail?

4. Which pop singer's career was resurrected after being featured by comic Peter Kay?

5. Who recorded "Ebony and Ivory" in 1982 with Paul McCartney?

6. Which eccentric pop singer made his mark with the band Culture Club?

7. Which pop singer starred alongside Kevin Costner in the film 'The Bodyguard'?

8. Which pop group's lead singer married the actress Gwyneth Paltrow?

*Answers on page 215*

# General Knowledge

1. What did the W stand for in the Name F W Woolworth?

2. What was advertised in the 1980's with the slogan 'If you see Sid, tell him?'

3. What was the last port of call for the Titanic?

4. Where is there an American flag that has not been lowered since 1969?

5. Which theoretical temperature corresponds to -273.15 degrees Celsius?

6. Which is the longest month in the year?

7. Chomolunga and Sagarmatha are alternative names for what?

8. What is the highest peak in England?

*Answers on page 215*

# Heart Attack!!!

One thing all landlords or ladies fear is the heart attack victim or someone dying on the premises. I know that sounds very unfeeling, but there is nothing like a heart attack victim to put someone off their mixed grill with extra fries and a pint of lager.

God forbid, if it's ever going to happen, it won't be on a quiet Tuesday in February, but bang in the middle of your busiest Friday night when, for once, everything is running smoothly

This particular nightmare began when one of the girls discreetly roared across the dining room.

"Phone for an ambulance, quick! This man's having a heart attack!"

Sure enough in the furthest and most inaccessible corner of the dining room, an extremely large man was obviously struggling with an apparent heart attack. His wife, poor soul, looked as if she was about to suffer one too and was endeavouring to get him to swallow some pills, but the man was by now, very distressed.

The ambulance crew arrived within minutes and on

assessing the situation, realised they had a problem. The dining room had both fixed tables and chairs and moveable tables and chairs; all laden with food and drink. Quite frankly, after the initial shock, most diners had resumed eating.

The problem was how to get him to the ambulance. He couldn't go out the front door on a stretcher; too many angles, he couldn't go via the fire escape for the same reason. It would have to be out through the kitchen.

Plates were shifted, drinks piled high on the bar, tables and chairs which could be moved were, but people were very protective of their food and very reluctant to let it go. However, with none too gentle persuasion, this was finally accomplished, and with the combined assistance of crew, staff and diners, the gentleman was rescued from his table and onto the stretcher.

With a great deal of pushing and heaving he made it to the kitchen. This accomplished, the diners lost all interest in the patient and were busy trying to retrieve their plates and drinks to resume their meals.

Everything now had to stop in the kitchen. Piles of crockery, food, in fact *everything* had to be moved out of the way.

Eventually he was passed over the kitchen equipment and out into to the waiting ambulance. The only thing the man on the stretcher seemed to care about was that he had been only halfway through his meal and my promise that when he was better, to come back as my guest seemed to cheer him up.

Meanwhile I was ungraciously thinking, for all this disruption, it had better not have been indigestion . . .

# What time is it???

The late drinker is the bane of every public house the length and breadth of the country. There is always one regular who appears ten minutes before closing and insists on having time to enjoy his drinks. On an odd occasion no one minds, or if the person is a shift worker, but the persistent late drinker is hard to tolerate.

We had a couple, Jill and Hugh, who arrived every evening at 10.45pm; fifteen minutes before close and at 11.45pm when we closed at midnight. Now, we were not their last port of call; they didn't work until late evening; they watched all the TV they wanted and then left their home at 10.30pm to walk to the pub.

The problem with the late drinker is, he has just begun his evening out and sees no reason why he can't enjoy his drink at whatever pace he wishes. He doesn't take into account that this particular hostelry has been open for twelve hours and that those working there would quite like to retire to their homes after a gruelling day.

Not only were these two late, but they were late and

boring, and I never quite worked out which was the greater sin; to be continually kept late, or to be kept late listening to the most inane rubbish. On arrival they would order their drinks and then, programme by programme, inform us what had happened.

Even though I have never been an exponent of the soaps, during their sojourn, I was well up to date. No mean feat, having never watched an episode. Heaven forbid I had taped a particular programme to watch at my leisure; no point. I got Jill's version and the programme lost its appeal after that.

Their second drink was timed with absolute precision. Just before time was called they would order their next drink, which was always a pint of lager and a bottle of something for him. A large white wine and glass of soda for her. This could extend their drinking time to almost double; she would sip her wine and with every sip add soda. The fecking glass never got empty and he would do the same. Sip of lager and top up with the bottle.

Now, licensing hours are very strictly adhered to and whilst a few minutes to get rid of customers at the weekend is overlooked, continually having customers on the premises at 11.30pm is not acceptable. Despite several warnings from the local Bobby, I could not shift this pair.

I tried everything to remedy the situation, but no joy. They 'knew their rights.' What about my rights? They refused to change their habits, so I had to resort to subterfuge.

Minutes before they arrived I changed the clock and advanced it by fifteen minutes with the assistance of the regulars around the bar, who had all advanced their watches too. So, on their arrival I had rung 'last orders'. Well, they argued and argued but we were adamant. Every pub opens by its clock and shuts by its clock. No contest.

This went on for a couple of nights and thinking they would beat me, they came in earlier. Problem solved! However, they left for pastures new soon after, telling everyone that they had not felt welcome. Christ – how long did that take to penetrate?

Their next 'home' was the pub across the road and believe me, I'm brave but I wouldn't tackle the publican from the Red Lion. I would watch them walking hand in hand, making for this hostelry but never later than 10pm.

# Last Drink . . .

Late one evening, two fairly sombre-looking men came into the bar. They ordered a couple of pints and sat down to enjoy them. Just then one of my locals came in and asked who had died. Thinking he had spotted the two chaps, I shushed him up.

"No, no," he said. "There's a bloody great hearse in the car park."

A few of his cronies rushed out to confirm this statement and sure enough, there *was* a bloody great hearse in the car park. After several more pints the sombre men explained they were on their way to Blackpool to collect their best pal who had died whilst on holiday. They regaled the assembled company with stories of their best mate and his antics and joined the locals in a first class piss up to commemorate their dear departed mate. Eventually, off they went to the local B&B to continue their journey the next day.

We all had a good laugh about the hearse and got on with the day. But lo and behold at about eight in the evening the hearse returned, complete with the body of their dear departed friend. They came into the pub and proceeded to get absolutely legless with the locals, saying that their friend would really appreciate it and this was the only way that they could do it.

I had terrors of the departed being propped up in his coffin in the corner of the bar with a pint but fortunately they left him in the hearse in the car park all night. I must admit I did check at various times to make sure he was still there.

Whether they had any other stops planned for their friend I will never know.

# Burnt Offering . . .

Just when you thought business couldn't get worse? Imagine how you'd feel if you saw your profits go up in smoke, quite literally, in the microwave!

One very busy Friday night one of my staff decided to empty the notes out of the till. For some reason, known only to her, she put them in the microwave for safekeeping. She took the plate of food which was already in there, out, and replaced it with the money. Locked the kitchen door and went back to work.

About ten minutes later, David, my husband, returning from a golf match, went into the kitchen to heat up his dinner which I had prepared earlier. Unfortunately, instead of a piping hot dinner, he had hundreds of pounds of burnt cash.

You try telling that to an insurance company!

# Fully booked . . .

Most publicans are paranoid about what the competition are doing and you will frequently be visited by other licensees on any pretext, just to see if you are doing better than they are. I have to say it was not a practice I indulged in myself (I always sent someone else!) But I could well understand their paranoia.

We were the busiest pub in town, no question, but I still had those pangs if perhaps, one rainy day, we were down one lunch on the week before. I would have staff haring all over the place checking numbers and faces. It probably took ten years for me to get it through my thick head that if we were quiet everyone else was dead.

Most of us publicans lived with the fact that sometimes someone else was a bit busier. But there were those who would go to any lengths to capture your punters and to sabotage your livelihood. One such scumbag almost ruined my whole Christmas trade. I have always been the trusting type, not so now. And when I first began serving evening meals one such gent set about stitching me up.

Our evening trade was limited to eight tables in our small dining room. It meant therefore that it was booked out very quickly and when we advertised our pre-Christmas menu, literally within two weeks we were fully booked. Unlike nowadays, no deposits were taken and confirmation was merely by telephone.

The first evening we were to serve Christmas fare we had thirty-six bookings and only four turned up. Now this was completely unheard of. As I said, we were famous for our food and although I was angry I did not smell a 'turkey' at that stage. The following evening, again we had thirty-six bookings and this time no one appeared.

I was devastated until I looked into the bar and there, with a gang of his cronies, was one of the worst publicans in town who seemed to be having a whale of a time. I'm nothing if not quick-witted and I was bloody sure he wasn't going to know his plan had worked. I made sure that the dining room door was closed, turned the music up full blast, made the chef bang as many pots and pans around as he could and look busy.

The girls were barging in and out of the room as if they were run off their feet. That bastard wouldn't laugh at me and get away with it. He was astounded. How could I be busy when they had filled the place with fictitious bookings? Of course, they couldn't ask. The bar was filling up with the usual Friday night mob and he had to get back to his own place but he was determined to find out what was going on.

We closed the side door so he couldn't see in and had staff stand immediately behind the door wearing paper hats and waving crackers around. I appeared as harassed as any busy, successful owner would be. We got away with it. But how to get through the rest of the month with virtually no bookings?

Well, as I said, we were the busiest and best place around and there are always people who don't book who were delighted to be accommodated. We got through it with no major losses.

As for him, well my time would come and he'd better watch out. But just as a little taster, the weekend before Christmas I phoned the brewery which happened to be the same as mine, and cancelled most of his order.

You try getting supplies at that time of the year – shame!

# Surf Rider

Theme nights used to be all the rage and I loved them. I would have the bar decked out for whatever theme it was, and the staff were always game for a laugh. We had Oscar night, Mediterranean nights, Thanksgiving; you name it we've had it.

One of the best was a Caribbean night which nearly cost me my pub and I'm sure we are still missing a customer or two. A major drinks company was looking for venues to launch a new rum. Well, I was always there with my hand out first. But to be fair, we were known to do things in style.

The deal was that they paid for most things, decorations, prizes etc . . . (music to my ears). Their downfall was in not giving me a budget! I took them at their word and decorated the bar as a Caribbean island (we even had sand, not the best idea). We had limbo dancing, fire-eaters (big mistake) and I had hired a surf board sideshow. Now I had never actually seen this, only a picture in a magazine, and it was like a bucking bronco, but a surf board. I had had lots of conversations with the people who were hiring it out.

The bar in which this event was being held was exceptionally long, not very wide, and in three sections. The section the Surf Rider was to be erected in was between the toilets and the main bar. Everything was set up. The DJ arrived early which was a first, and people were pouring in. I had ordered a hundred coconuts to serve drinks in, but one of my stupid staff had pierced each end to get the milk out and of course, having spent most of the afternoon sawing them in half, couldn't work out why the punch was spewing out the bottom. However, not deterred, we used them to serve the food in. It was bloody awful but after the amount of rum the buggers had drunk, no one noticed or if they did no one said anything.

All my staff were game for anything but the two I could always count on to get things going were working on the 'Meet and Greet' table. I have always worked on the principle of 'never assume anything' so I should have known better. When they asked if they could have a couple of drinks to get them in the mood I should not, of course, have assumed that that was what they would have. Everyone who came in was given a fairly potent Caribbean Cocktail, featuring the new rum. Guess what? These two buggers had one along with them. Half an hour after the party started they were under the 'Meet and Greet' table, out for the count!

The limbo dancing competition was brilliant but was won by a fifteen year old girl who was promptly thrown out for being under age and I saved on one of the prizes.

The fire-eater would have been good, if he hadn't set most of the decorations on fire and some idiot then tried to put the flames out by throwing the punch over them. Christ, it was like an inferno and we were lucky the whole place didn't go up, but most of the punters thought it was some new pyrotechnics, and part of the show.

The Grand Finale was to be the Surf Rider and people had been queuing most of the night. I knew as soon as I saw it we were doomed, but the two eejits in charge had also been on the rum punch and they didn't know if it was New York or New Year and despite my protests, continued to inflate this fucking great monstrosity.

Oh, it fitted in the space alright, completely, absolutely. No one could get in or out. Those in the toilets were there for the foreseeable future and those who weren't, had to dance cross-legged for quite some time. God alone knows what had happened but the valve had stuck and it could not be deflated.

Well, I had about ten customers trapped in the loo and they were getting antsy. The main door was blocked and I nearly had a bloody riot on my hands with drunken teenagers wanting to have a go. Have a go? I'd bloody have a go at them!

The eejits had retired to their van and I could see only one way out. I let everyone on, stilettos, the lot, and within five minutes it was deflated. So were the eejits when they realised they weren't getting paid and the Surf Rider had ridden its last wave.

Everyone thought it had been a fantastic night. The drinks company were delighted at the amount I had sold. Then they got the PR bill and I think that took the edge off it! I nearly had a nervous breakdown and the two 'meet and greeters'? We all forgot about them and at 2.30 in the morning I had to go back to the pub and let them out when they set the bloody alarms off.

See what I mean, check everywhere!

# Striking Terror . . .

I have always picked staff for their personality rather than ability or experience. I can always give them ability and experience. All my girls were lookers; lookers with attitude. They could handle themselves in the bar and give as good as they got.

The guys, well they shouldn't have attitude but should certainly be able to handle themselves. Everyone had to have fun while working and make the experience for the customer so good they wanted to come back. Now that's what it says in the manual. The reality was, yes, they were all good looking but the attitude always seemed to be towards me. What the hell did I do? Except give them a job.

They squabbled and bitched about everything. One had cut too many lemon slices, one had not cut enough lemon slices. One collected the last glasses, no, the other had collected the last glasses; that drink was for me, no, it was bought for me, and so on and so on.

For all the back-biting and squabbling, believe it or not they were all good pals and socialised together regularly. Not a good situation for me; if one had a hangover, they all had hangovers.

But we did have some memorable nights out. We must be the only people to be barred from our country's capital city. It wasn't our fault really. How were we to know that all the soldiers and police officers weren't practising for the Edinburgh Tattoo?

We had been on a city tour; the one with the Ghouls and Ghosties when we decided we'd had enough history and would rather go for a drink. Some bright spark said they knew a short cut through the castle and off we all trotted.

Now the obvious thing to do when taking a short cut through the main tourist attraction in Scotland is to dodge from pillar to pillar, pretending to be Ninjas.

I am sure the security guards were being extra vigilant: for gawd's sake how many terrorists dress up in stilettos and short skirts? Mind you, that was the guys, you should have seen what the girls were wearing.

We were having great fun and yes, we did hear public announcement messages but paid no attention to them; after all we were just taking a short cut. Right in the middle of the esplanade, all the security lights went on; it was like Wembley at a Take That concert. There were police, soldiers, armed vehicles and half a dozen fierce-looking dogs.

"Hit the ground!" screamed a big guy with a loud-hailer.

"What the fuuuuuuuuck?"

"Hit the ground"

"Fuck off ya nutter!" shouted one of the girls "Ah've got Dolce Gabana jeans on!"

"We're just gaun tae Deacon Brodie's!" shouted another.

"Hit the ground, NOW!"

"Hit the ground or we'll open fire!"

"Ya fucker, he's no jokin'"

It seemed they really did want us to 'hit the ground'. So fifteen of us did and were immediately surrounded by half the country's armed forces. It's amazing how quickly you sober up when some big bugger shoves the barrel of a gun up your nose.

It appeared that the Queen took great exception to a few of her subjects carousing through her castle and playing hide and seek on the esplanade. Miserable old trout. What harm were we doing? And no one, *no one* could think for one moment that any self respecting terrorist would go out terrorising, dressed in D&G jeans, fake Laboutin shoes and a brand new Louis Vuitton bag bought from the market that day. Fucking idiots!

Well, we were ceremoniously shoved on the number 44 Port Seton bus and told not to come back. So we are the only people I know to be barred from Edinburgh.

I will say that when I have to go shopping in town, I fool them. I take the train to Glasgow and then back to Edinburgh, just in case!

# Life's a Bitch!

"She's got too many shifts next week."
"I can't work that many shifts next week."
"I don't want any shifts next week."

"Can I get away early tonight?"
"She got away early last night!"
"I'm not working tonight!"

"Can I borrow your car tomorrow?"
"She borrowed David's car last week!"
"I'm learning to drive!"

"Can I get an advance this week?"
"She got an advance last week!"
"Why haven't I got any wages this week?"

"I want to go on holiday this week."
"She went on holiday last week!"
"Why can't *I* go on holiday?"


"COS YOU'RE A FUCKING CUSTOMER!!!"

# The Writing on the Wall

Graffiti was another time-consuming problem. Mind you, it was better than any gossip column. Taking a squint at the door in the Ladies would always keep you abreast of who was doing what to whom, and where. Comical though this was, the job was a bit like painting the Forth Bridge, never-ending. You had no sooner either washed all the offending remarks off or repainted the door when it would all re-appear as if by magic.

I have never caught anyone writing on a toilet door, but I will admit to once, and only once, doing it myself. Whilst in the powder room of a neighbouring hostelry, I read a comment about one of my customers who I really disliked. He had recently split from his long-time girlfriend and I'm sure either she or one of her sisters wrote:

*Michael ***** has genital warts* to which I added, using my best eye liner pencil:

*Yep, but they are on his nose.*

To this day I giggle every time I see him.

# Graffiti

Beauty is only a light switch away.

A dirty mind is a terrible thing to waste.

Don't blame me, I'm from Uranus.

Earth is full. Go home.

Here I am! Now what are your other two wishes?

I did a drot of lugs in college, I hink I thave dain bramage

Can I lick the bowl? Shut up and flush.

I'm not your type. I'm not inflatable.

# . . . And more

Avoid Hangovers; Stay Drunk

Can't Feed 'Em! Don't Breed 'Em!

Conserve toilet paper - use both sides.

Constipated People Don't Give A Shit.
Don't f*** with my head and I won't think with my dick!

I used up all my sick days so I called in dead!

Don't beam me up yet Scotty I'm having a sh**

# I'm a Celebrity . . .

Dennis billed himself as the TV chef and no matter how many times we told him, that no, he was a just a chef who had been on TV, we couldn't change his mind. Or alter his star billing. Actually he had appeared twice on TV. The first was as a contestant on the Weakest Link and how he got through the interview baffles us to this day. He is thick.

As anyone knows, to go off first in such a competition is most embarrassing, and guess what? Dennis not only went off first but was voted off by every single contestant including himself, another first! He wasn't on long enough to be insulted by Ann but that was no deterrent to our boy. Oh no! He'd been on the telly and was now star struck. He knew he was 'a natural'.

This took place around the time that TV chefs were becoming the new 'A-listers', and Dennis saw himself up there alongside the Gordon Ramsays and Jamie Olivers. If the truth be told he looked more like Fanny Craddock than either of these two but they were no better nor worse chefs than him. And you know the old saying 'God loves a trier'. Dennis was certainly going to give it his best shot.

He had a plan. What was it? Simply bombard every single show about to be recorded with applications, and he did. His tenacity got him a slot on a new show called 'Wife Swap'. Absolutely nothing to do with his cooking skills, but putting his wife and family under the microscope.

Dennis was certainly not a 'new man' nor a 'metro' one as they were being called then. Deodorant was for poofs and his wife was there to do his bidding.

The theory behind the show was that two families swapped the heads of the households (the wives) for two weeks and the show would pinpoint their shortcomings. Their shortcomings? In his case there were nothing *but* shortcomings. He didn't appear to have one redeeming feature.

Dennis' recording was the first in the series and had huge press coverage before it was aired. He arranged an after show party for all his family and friends. Everyone was as excited as he was and wanted to share in his glory. All, that is, except Debbie his wife. She had hated the whole experience and learned a lot about her life that she didn't like, and she had every intention of changing it. Number one to be changed was Dennis but he didn't know it yet!

The show was a triumph for the network, for the ratings, for the town. But sadly, not for Dennis and Debbie. He didn't, and still doesn't realise what a prat he made of himself. She, on the other hand, systematically changed every bad thing in her life. Finally the wife swapped, yep! She swapped her husband for a producer she'd met on the show. The irony is that because of the new husband's work, *she* goes to all the A-list parties and meets all those people Dennis so longed to rub shoulders with.

But Dennis is a legend in his own mind and for a small town, as near to celebrity status as most of us are likely to get. And let's face it, he wasn't bad for business.

There are still people who will come in just to meet the TV chef, not many, but a few . . .

# Riding lessons . . .

Being married had never hampered Dennis' pursuit of women, so being single changed nothing. But, he was a 'five minutes to closing' kinda guy. He would literally, five minutes before the last bell, spy any woman not obviously attached and go in for the kill. It always worked and he seldom had to buy them a drink. But oh, he captured some horrors. I know this is sexist but there is no other way to describe Dennis' conquests.

Most pubs have a Sunday club and we were no exception. The die-hards would congregate on Sunday morning to cure their hangovers and to carry out the post mortem of the night before. Dennis was always first to arrive and always his conquests were featured, without exception.

However, this particular morning, although he was first to arrive he was very subdued. Thinking his hangover to be worse than usual, I gave him a double shot of Jagermeister (our tried and tested remedy). The rest of the cronies dribbled in and the post mortem of the previous night's escapades began. Dennis was unusually quiet and reticent about his antics despite being repeatedly quizzed. It was the consensus of opinion that for once he had failed to score. If only!

About an hour into the session, he looked like he'd seen a ghost; he jumped up, gave a girlie squeal and bolted to his kitchen. What the hell? There, standing at the bar was an elderly woman, and I mean elderly. She looked like she'd had a helluva hard paper round and held a riding crop in her hand.

"Is Dennis in?" she coyly asked, well as coyly as any seventy year old could (honest!).

"No," says I. "He doesn't work on a Sunday."

"Will he be in later?"

"Not sure," I replied, trying to stifle a laugh and glaring at those not trying so hard.

"Oh, well. He left this at mine this morning," slamming the riding crop on the bar.

It took almost an hour to persuade him to come out and face the music.

A riding crop. I shudder to think.

# Extremely so!

The advent of extreme sports has taken the country completely by storm and surprise. It is not uncommon to see guys leaping across stairwells and flying across basement areas. Even the most unlikely characters indulge in these pastimes. Before, we would have just called it *'being pissed'* and *'a hazardous journey home'*. Not so now.

We had two experts in this hobby. The two Lees. Lee number one was a cyclist. He spent almost 90% of his free time on, under, or lying beside his bike. It was his absolute pride and joy. He stripped it down daily. Washed, polished and re-assembled it. Strangely, he always had a few nuts and bolts left over.

Now this guy could go at the speed of light; he would pedal for all he was worth and every junction or red light was a challenge. He constantly battled against the traffic and always had to be first away. He would take on everything, from a Smart Car to a Ferrari but . . . he was a danger to himself and to every other road user as he had absolutely no fear and usually no brakes. Remember the extra nuts and bolts.

It was his ambition to compete in the Tour de France. He would have more chance in a Tour de Farce. Lee number one went everywhere on his bike, absolutely everywhere and if he was a danger when sober, can you imagine what he was like after a few beers?

Lee number two was a skateboard freak. Since receiving his first board when he was a lowly seven, he had never walked anywhere again. Like Lee number one, his boards were his pride and joy. He had them in all shapes and sizes, all colours and creeds. He had competition boards, exhibition boards and boards from Argos. Seriously, he had common or garden boards that were for taking the dog for a walk. Yes, the dog had a board too. He had a board for going to the off-licence and even a tandem board in case he ever got lucky.

While Lee number one was a danger to road users, Lee number two was a danger to everyone else. They pretty much endangered the total population of the town between them. Wasn't I the lucky one to have them as regulars?

The journey to the pub was always an adventure. They would synchronize watches, leave at the same time and using some peculiar handicap system, race to the bar; the loser buying the first round.

During the evening they would have a beer then race round the town, starting and finishing at the pub door, annihilating everything in their wake. As the night wore on they grew more and more reckless. Wheels came off, people were knocked to the ground and it wasn't unusual to see them going hell for leather, sparks flying, with a baying mob after them.

It was time to do something. The previous evening, being absolutely pissed, Lee number two went hurtling through the beer garden, over the fence and into the garden next door. Unfortunately our neighbours were having a barbeque and didn't appreciate having an idiot on a three-wheeled skateboard, (he had managed to lose a wheel), land in their ornamental pool. This was followed by a crash and the sound of breaking glass, his BFF had failed to stop yet again, (remember the nuts and bolts) and had crashed into the side of their conservatory. Thankfully no-one was hurt except them, but they didn't count. Something definitely had to be done.

I had been warned by the licensing police that these two came under the same laws as any drink driver and I could be held responsible. I was at my wit's end. What could be done with this maniacal pair?

Let's look at the situation. Here we had two single blokes in their late 20's; both reasonably good looking, both intelligent (well that's debatable), both popular, so what was missing? What would stop them racing round the town like a couple of 'Road Runners' on acid? What would calm them down? Who would stop the feckers ruining my good name with the police? A woman. But not just any woman.

I had to come up with someone so fit she would stop this pair in their tracks. But how? Where was I going to get a stunner (or preferably two) who would understand their enthusiasm for speed and danger but would keep it in check? I have to say for once I was stumped.

This is where fate lent a hand. Edinburgh during the Festival is buzzing with life and excitement and people from all walks of life. And we always enjoyed a big night out in town during this time. Starting with a show and then basically drinking our way from 'Princes Street to Oblivion'.

This year we had chosen to go see 'The He-She's from Taiwan'. Now this show was fantastic. It was fabulous, funny and went at such a pace. And the stars of the show were two 'Roller-Skating Divas', two of the most gorgeous creatures imaginable. The two Lee's were hooked. Completely and utterly hooked. What more could a bloke ask for? The most stunning, sexy girls . . . and wheels!

For the next four weeks they spent every night at the show and joined the cast afterwards to party, and this crowd could party. I was never sure if at this stage they actually knew what a He-She was. But, hey ho! They weren't kids and our town was quieter and much safer without the marauding wheelers.

But, all good things come to an end and the Festival was wrapping up. Dear God, the thought of them coming back, and heartbroken at that, didn't bear thinking about. But were we in for a shock.

On the last night of the show, we were visited by two most exotic creatures, dressed in oriental lycra and vaguely familiar.

"We've just come to say goodbye," said the smaller of the two.

"Goodbye? Hello would be a start!" says I.

"Don't say you don't recognise us?"

Jesus, it's not often I'm stumped for words, but standing before me were, yes, you've guessed it! The two newest cast members of the 'He-She's from Taiwan' and very ladylike they were too . . .

Now that's what you call "Extreme".

# Team Games

The traditional pub games: cribbage, bar skittles, dominoes and darts are very much in decline and have been taken over by pool and Wii nights. However, the older style pubs still maintain domino and darts teams and if you ask any publican, they are the bane of his life, especially the Women's Darts Team. The ladies team consists of a pool of about fifteen women and if you study these teams across the country you will find their make up is in exactly the same proportions, but with differing accents.

Firstly, there are the Captain and Vice-Captain. These two pseudo-lezzies have absolute power over the rest of their team-mates and always, always dress the same way. Jeans from the market, usually two pairs for a fiver. (One to wear and one to wash). A sweat shirt in winter and a polo shirt in summer with, of course, the team name or logo. These garments were usually bought when a new licensee took over and they conned him or her into spending a couple of hundred pounds on the promise of all their business. It is quite easy therefore, to work out how long the present landlord has been in residence. Check the colour chart for the fade factor.

Back to the team. We have the two top dogs then we have four or five veterans, who have been team members since before the league started and now, if ever, couldn't hit a barn door at twenty paces. Why? Their eyes have gone, their aim has gone and usually after a couple of halfs, they're gone. However, they are still an integral part of the team: they can keep score and they know the drinks round off by heart. Usually they bring their knitting and are of the opinion that 'darts night gets you away from *him* for a night'.

The next four or five are normally daughters of the veterans, usually single mums who can play reasonably well. After all, they cut their back teeth on a 'Tungsten Double Barrel Arrow' and were fed crisps and coke from the time they were weaned. These women are the backbone of any darts team. They dress similarly to their mothers but without the team logo. Usually a sweatshirt from JB Sport's sale which is invariably navy or black, (think kids), and trainers from the market. They gossip about their kids, offers on at the supermarket and on darts night the main topic of conversation is the Tart. The highlight of their year is the team weekend away which they save for religiously.

Finally, we have the Tart and her two fat pals. Every team has this combination. The two fat lassies are the publican's delight. They can consume a box of crisps before the grub goes out at half time and have a drink or ten. They are in their early twenties, work in the local fish filleting plant and Tuesday night is their main night out. They are close pals with the final member of the team, who epitomises glamour and everything they wish they were. We shouldn't call her a tart but she is always on the prowl and her uniform is very different from the rest of the group. She wears skinny jeans, skimpy glittery tops and always, heels, make-up to perfection and big hair. A look she perfected fifteen years ago and has never seen the need to change.

So that's the team and be it a home or away, the line up for both teams is exactly the same. Darts night takes the same format, week in week out. All members arrive at around 7pm, except for the Tart. She is always late: the babysitter didn't arrive, or the cunt of an ex-husband was late, or one of the kids was missing. There is a reason for this. First on the agenda is the paying of subs, outing money and raffle tickets. She knows the two fat lassies will divvy up for her and she'll settle up later. Of course she seldom does but the fat pals are so delighted to be her chosen two, they don't mind paying for the privilege. Of course the rest of the team get mad about this, but to no avail, her posse is united.

They are a fairly good team and win more than they lose. During the course of the night they separate into little groups, gossiping, chatting and generally having a good evening, but the Tart circles round the bar. If there's a men's darts team in the other bar, she has won a watch: drinks paid for all evening and she just nips back and forth between her crowd and the guys. She has it down to perfection and there are very few nights she doesn't go home with a trophy; nothing to do with darts.

But all this is simply practice for the 'Big One'. Every year the girls go off to Blackpool for a weekend darts tournament. They save weekly for this outing and usually have enough for travel, accommodation and spending money and the chant for that week is:

"What happens in Blackpool stays in Blackpool!"

Really, the only one this proverb applies to is the Tart. The most exciting thing that any of the others could lay claim to is dodging the bill for all of them at the 'All You Can Eat Buffet'. Fifteen go in and twelve pay. She, on the other hand, is in her element. It's a mixed tournament and she, and a couple of dozen others of her ilk have free rein with approximately two hundred guys.

The team arrives early on Saturday morning at the Tower Ballroom and fight tooth and nail for one of the best tables.

They have a well-planned strategy for securing their table. Near the toilets but not too near. Near the bar but not too near. Near the food outlets and for the two fat pals this can't be too near. Having come to this venue for ten years they know table 214 is the best and table 214 is their goal. Most years they secure it and this year was no exception. The main feature about table 214 is the view. It is a 'see and be seen' table and if there are any matches televised then our team is the one seen all over the country. For the Tart this is the nearest to 'A-list Celebrity' she's going to get.

The Captain and Vice Captain organise with almost military precision; everyone has their job to ensure the team are catered for. To curtail costs, lunch is provided courtesy of the breakfast table. Each member has to secure a buttered roll, a boiled egg, a slice of cheese and a banana. This way, only drinks require to be bought.

Unfortunately the two fat lassies spoiled it for the rest of them last year by almost clearing the breakfast buffet table and wrapping their ill-gotten goods in a checked tablecloth. This year they were given absolute instructions and woe betide them if they got caught again. The two fat lassies were not happy bunnies but were too afraid to disobey orders. So to compensate for a light lunch they ate their way through the breakfast buffet which of course left a shortage for the lunch plunder by the other team members. So they were in the dog house again.

Not wanting to spoil the outing and to make amends for their misdemeanour, the fat lassies offered to do the first shift of table watching. This was to ensure that no one nicked their stuff and more importantly, no one nicked their table. At all times, except when the team were playing, someone had to remain in situ. Whilst a team were in play, officials looked after their belongings. This had come about after a gang of Eastern Europeans had plundered the venue by simply waiting in the wings till a team went forward to play, leaving their table empty. They walked off with the lot.

The Captain and Vice Captain wandered off to meet other big lezzies. The single mums went off to look for prezzies. The veterans just headed for the bar and the Tart went on the prowl. She was a free agent: usually the two fat lassies held her back, always needing the loo, needing a drink, having a snack. But today she could cruise on her own, observe and mark out the talent and the competition.

Over the years she had made a few enemies amongst the other tarts, but so what? She could handle herself. Wow! What was that on the starboard side? The most amazing looking guy she'd ever seen. He was gorgeous, but shit! It was only her absolute worst enemy hanging round his neck. These two had had a bit of a skirmish last year and our tart had certainly taken second prize. But her enemy was looking a bit the worse for wear, had put on a bit of weight and wasn't looking as fit as before. Weighing up the situation she decided she would go for it. But not now, time to shine on another stage.

The team were ready to play, flexing knuckles, limbering up, throwing a few arrows, all except the fat lassies. They had been left for far longer than they'd expected and gotten a little peckish, so what were they to do? They couldn't go off for a hot dog or a burger so they had eaten their lunch a bit early. Ten thirty to be precise. But someone must have come and stolen the rest when they weren't looking.

Fuck! Where was it? Where were the eggs, the bananas and the rolls? Oh shit! Should they make a run for it? Fuck! Run? They couldn't move! In fact they were stuck, they couldn't get out from the table. The team Captain and the Vice Captain were looming. What the fuck were they going to do? With one almighty crash, the thinner of the two fat lassies managed to free them from their predicament. Off they went to play.

The team performed brilliantly and for the first time they were through to the next round. Going back to table 214 the TV cameras were focused on them and they shone. The two big lezzies spoke glowingly about their team mates. The veterans answered technical questions succinctly and cleverly, the single mums smiled and joked with the presenter and the two fat lassies were the heroines of the game. The only one not on the telly was the Tart. She'd seen her opportunity to snatch Mr. Gorgeous and she wasn't letting this one get away.

The team got a bye into the next round and looked like they had a chance to get to the semis. Never before in the history of the town had any team gotten this far and they were ecstatic. Pep talk from the captain. No more booze and forget food till after the semis. The two fat lassies couldn't believe their luck. Instead of being drummed out of the team they were actually being congratulated for disposing of the food and temptation. They, of course, were starving but were taking no chances.

While all this was going on the Tart had gone in for the kill and, in a very romantic broom cupboard, had her wicked way with Mr. Gorgeous; just a quickie, but that would do for now. She had plans for him. How good would they look together on the telly? She could see the cover of OK magazine.

They won the semis easily and couldn't believe it. The Finals, the Finals. They were in the Finals!

The Team Captain and Vice Captain treated them to a slap-up meal at Harry Ramsden's. A Fish 'n' Chip Tea. The fat lassies got extras on the side and no one said a thing. With strict instructions – no booze and an early night – the party headed back to the caravan site. Next year they would stay in the Excelsior if they won the cup. Just imagine, the Excelsior!

The two big lezzies were dreaming of appearing on Bullseye, the veterans, of en-suite bathrooms in the Excelsior, and the single mums, of the Champions Dinner Dance. The two fat lassies dreamt about a free 'All You Can Eat Buffet' and the Tart? Well she wasn't dreaming, in fact, she wasn't even asleep. She was making use of all her time with Mr. Gorgeous who turned out to be the new British Darts Champion.

Well, she *had* thought he looked vaguely familiar.

The day of the finals dawned bright and sunny and the team assembled in the breakfast room. The Team Captain and Vice Captain, together with most of the staff, were watching carefully what each team member was eating. Leaving nothing to chance they requested a proper packed lunch, no nicking anything from the buffet. They could be 'The Winners' and had to show a bit of class.

No sign of the Tart. Christ! Where was she? They scoured the caravan site, phoned her mobile which was turned off, and reluctantly left for the venue. If she didn't show up they were scuppered. The team had to consist of the same members for each match and you could hardly miss her.

*Pleeeeezzze* make her be early and be at the Tower. *Pleeeze* make her turn up. Every one of the team members prayed all the way there that she'd be sitting waiting for them. This was their big chance, surely she wouldn't let them down? It was ten minutes till match time, everyone was buzzing; the TV cameras were swinging round the venue but kept returning to them. Table 214 was a prime spot. The team captain and vice captain were pacing up and down. The veterans were in a state, the single mums were tearing up and down looking for her and the two Fat Pals were systematically working their way through the packed lunches. Comfort Eating.

Here she was, oh my God, here she was; she was

here. Oh! My! God!

Wearing last night's clothes, last night's make up and hair like a divot, she certainly wasn't 'A-list' material. But the important thing was the match. They were contenders. They could win – not could – *would*. The atmosphere was electric, they were one up, then two down, then equal and so it went on. Point for point, everyone was at the top of their game. Yesterday's gear and bad hairdos didn't matter a damn.

It was the last game and the team captain was on. She played like the captain she was, not like a big lezzie but as a sportsman and gave it her all. The place erupted, they'd won! They'd actually won! Oh my God, oh my God, oh my God! They were jumping, shouting, screaming; party poppers, champagne, (Asti Spumante.) It was absolute madness.

Next came . . . the Presentation . . . the cameras, the speeches, the cup, it was sheer bedlam. Eventually they made their way back to table 214 and out the corner of her eye the Tart could see Mr. Gorgeous but oh fuck! Who was back hanging round his neck? The enemy she'd seen off the day before.

Mr Gorgeous was there in his capacity as British Dart's Champion and he was to interview them. The team were in their element. Everyone, that is except the Tart. She was fuming, she was absolutely fucking speechless. She'd just helped her team win the biggest prize in Dart World and here he was, the arse-hole she'd shagged all night (and he was rubbish), being pawed in public by that fat horror.

She couldn't resist any longer, she was a street fighter, she knew how to handle herself and, with one almighty swipe, she decked the bugger. How dare he! How fucking dare he! And what was that fat slapper screaming about her husband? Whose husband? What husband? And come to think of it the fat slapper wasn't fat, she was pregnant. Oh fuck!

What happens in Blackpool stays in Blackpool, but not when it's televised . . .

# Double or Quits

Lily had been working in the pub for five or six years when I took over and she was one of the best barmaids we ever had. We were the same age and had gone to school together. Whilst we had never been buddies, we knew each other fairly well.

To say I was shocked when I met her for the first time in years, is an understatement. She was so old looking; I mean we were both in our 40's, but she had pure white hair, never wore make-up and certainly looked much older than her years. Why? Because she had the ultimate control freak for a husband. But she was a great barmaid; everyone loved Lily, everyone that is except her husband Seamus. He was a dour, peculiar man who watched Lily like a hawk.

Now I have to say he did have cause to watch her, she was a bit of a girl. But he was such a pain, we all covered up for her. Seamus was convinced that Lily couldn't handle her drink. He was always on her case and checking her out. What he didn't know was exactly how much Lily did drink, and why it looked like she couldn't handle it.

As I've said she was very popular and was bought loads of drinks throughout her shift. What she would do was every time someone bought her a drink, she would pour a measure of vodka into a pint glass. We had strict rules about drinking while on duty and it was instant dismissal if I caught anyone. Lily knew the rules and obeyed them.

At the end of her shift she could have as many as ten vodkas in her glass. She then topped it up with coke and quite blatantly sat there drinking her pint of coke, to quench her thirst! They would always have a couple before heading home, so to bulk up her intake, we had a system. Lily would go off to the toilet; on passing the bar whoever was working would pass her a large vodka and coke, which she would drink on the way to the loo.

She would leave the glass in the toilet and pass the money over on her way back. This could happen three or four times in the hour that they were in. By this time Seamus would think she had had a pint of coke and three vodka and cokes, and he would be furious and shouting about the state of her. Lily would be almost comatose, but so would you be, after something like sixteen vodkas in the space of about an hour. We all knew it was foolhardy but it was Lily, and he was a plonker.

She was not against a few extra-maritals either. I can't count the number of times we found her tights or knickers hanging from the flag pole or stuffed in the wheelie bin and again, although it was wrong, everyone covered up for her, just to outwit him.

The one thing which always puzzled Seamus was that she never got drunk while on holiday, and he adamantly refused to believe that foreign drink was as strong as the booze we sold. He would proclaim to anyone listening, that his Lily could have three or four in their local on a Saturday and be legless, but she could drink four times that amount on holiday and still be able to sing on the karaoke and stagger home. So it was obvious that the foreign muck wasn't as potent.

This situation continued for many years. She would work the Saturday afternoon shift, finish at seven, have her bucket load of vodkas and be carried home and he never suspected. Until, that is, he went down with some dreadful lurgy. The doctor put him on a course of antibiotics which meant, as everyone knows, he couldn't have a drink. So when he came to collect Lily on Saturday evening, instead of his usual lager he had a pint of coke.

There they were: sitting side by side drinking coke when the barmaid signalled to Lily that she had her first drink lined up. Off she trotted to the loo. While she was gone, Seamus, having finished his coke, and being a miserable devil, decided to finish off hers. It nearly blew his fucking hat off. There had to be a mistake, how the hell was he drinking neat vodka? Whoa! The penny dropped and everything fell into place. It dawned on him why she couldn't handle her drink, he'd put it down to her getting older; as if! But what was worse was, we were all in on the joke and he was not amused.

Unfortunately, that was the last shift she was ever allowed to work. We all missed her, but maybe her liver wouldn't have stood much more!

# All bets are off . . .

Over the years we've had several staff with drink problems. Let's face it the last place someone with a drink problem should work is a bar. But it's a bit of a chicken and egg situation.

We had one dishwasher who shook so badly we had to give her a half lager before she started work just to cut down on breakages. She'd come in half an hour early and we'd give her her drink with a straw as she couldn't hold the glass without spilling most of it. By the time she had consumed her drink, at 8.30 in the morning, she was on the road to recovery and the dishes were fairly safe.

Then there was Marilyn. Marilyn had worked in nearly every bar in town and been sacked from most of them, but she was a fantastic barmaid. She was stunning and was the epitome of a barmaid. Tall, blond, voluptuous and had a way with her that made husbands drool, but strangely, wives liked her too. Probably because they felt sorry for her. I actually never knew how drunk she was, till I met her sober!

She had a following and I *mean* a following.

Wherever Marilyn was working, there her fans would gather; and they could spend, never any trouble, just party night every night. Of course I knew her background and was loath to take her on, but she was such a lovely girl and of course, she promised me that this time it was different. Of course it wasn't.

Rumour had it that she'd start the day with a large port and brandy. A lethal combination at any time, but with cornflakes! This was her livener for the day. After that she could put on her slap, get dressed, and believe it or not, drive. She would always arrive at least fifteen minutes before her shift was to start and she'd have the bar set up to perfection. Nothing was left to chance and she checked and checked she had everything. I have to say I found it a bit OTT. Absolutely everything was within arm's reach. When this was done, she'd have a strong black coffee with a large brandy in it (this one took a while to suss out). She was ready to face her public.

Most pubs are fairly quiet in the mornings but we served food from breakfast onwards, so everyone had to be on their toes and Marilyn was good, up to a point. She would batter through lunchtime, serving drinks, taking orders, making up bills and because she had everything to hand she was on top of her game. For exactly four hours.

Then, like a switch being thrown, the booze would either kick in, or wear off and it would all go to hell. If the lunchtime crowd lingered we were well and truly fucked. People got charged twenty quid for a bowl of soup and others who were paying for four lunches and drinks got charged two pounds. She usually finished off her cabaret by plunging head first into the cellar while carrying a full tray of drinks.

No matter how many times she fell down there, she never broke as much as a finger nail. She seemed to have the 'Drunk Man's Roll' down to an art form.

While all this was going on the other staff and the customers would cover up for her. How did I not see this? Well, I was stuck in the kitchen frying fish or some other delicacy. Sure I would hear commotion but seldom got free of the fryer quick enough to find out what was going on. By the time I was cleared up Marilyn had finished her shift; the till was cashed up (by someone else) and she had had a large brandy to calm her down. So, a bit like Lily's husband, I never really sussed out what was going on.

However, things were getting to the point where guys were coming in just to see her perform. Her gymnastics were becoming legendary and there was a book being run on how long she'd last – 5/1. When she'd break a limb – 10/1. And the big one: when she'd take someone else down with her – 33/1. Hell mend the buggers, they had to pay it all out on one day and what a fiasco that turned out to be.

The only way I could tell how drunk she was, was by using the lipstick test. When she was sober her make-up was perfect. As the booze took hold she would re-apply her lipstick, mirror free, and just purse her lips. But as she got more and more pissed, her aim got worse and worse and she ended up looking like something from Billy Smart's Circus, with lipstick from nose to chin.

The day she finished off, the amateur bookmakers started fairly quietly. She had obviously been hammered the night before and the hangover was kicking in as she skittered round the bar getting it ready for the onslaught. I should have noticed that her coffee had been poured as soon as she came in and by now she was on her second and it wasn't doing the trick. The crowds started piling in and very soon she was in a mess, orders all over the place, wrong drinks and general mayhem.

Although the customers and the staff loved her, when you have only got half an hour for lunch she lost some of her appeal. She had already fallen down the cellar twice and instead of sympathy, she was getting abuse. One guy had seen his pint disappear three times and he was not the most patient of men.

The other girls were trying to help her but she had got herself in such a muddle that it was nigh on impossible. It had got to the stage that customers were having to put their hands up when someone called out what was on the plate. Some were so hungry and desperate they were claiming anything just to get fed. This was causing arguments in the bar, where more than half a dozen diners were almost coming to blows over a steak and kidney pie, which promptly landed on the floor with all the pushing and pulling.

Then disaster struck. Barrel needed changing; she opened the cellar hatch and promptly fell down it. Didn't tell the other girl working on the bar; *she* went down like a sack of potatoes and the pot lifter followed suit. Christ there were more bodies in the cellar than in the bar. To this day I don't know how someone wasn't killed.

The clever buggers had to pay out on all bets. One, she'd broken her little finger; two, she'd taken two staff with her and yes, she was sacked.

Okay, we missed the extra income from her following but given the number of glasses she broke in a shift we almost broke even.

# Bare-faced cheek . . .

Next door to the pub was a very stylish hairdressing salon, owned and run by the most flamboyant person I have ever met. Clive Eastwood: known to everyone as Tint. Tint, his three top stylists, Perm, Clipper and Tina the Tranny treated our bar as an extension of their salon. It wasn't unusual to see a lady, head full of perm curlers, sipping on a G&T.

Tint almost defied description. He looked like a cross between Jimmy Saville and Dolly Parton. He was six feet tall with long blond tresses, more gold than the National Reserve and clad from top to toe in a white leather jumpsuit. He was magnificent.

Now, Tina the Tranny wasn't. She wasn't a tranny. But she definitely looked more butch than the other three and because she was such a big girl, was always mistaken for a man in drag, especially given the company she kept. Perm and Clipper were just mini replicas of Tint. They dressed like him but the effect was more romper suit than jumpsuit.

Whilst this crowd used the bar like their own private club, it was mostly during working hours and early evening. Their real socializing was in town; either in the gay bars or the top venues. It was very seldom that they came in contact with the young set who frequented the bar in the evening or at weekends. Quite frankly this was a blessing; I don't think our provincial little town was ready for them. Their dress code was definitely 'if it doesn't shock, it doesn't work', and believe me, they shocked.

On a very rare occasion they would meet up with friends and then go into town but they were normally off the premises before anyone paid them any attention However, on the evening of their staff night out they were certainly noticed.

As usual, they had claimed their special corner which gave them a grand view of the Saturday night crowd who resembled extras from the Star Wars Café, and these raucous hairdressers were having the time of their life. This however, was not going down well with the locals.

About an hour after they arrived one of them, either Perm or Clipper, made a move to go to the gents. As he proceeded through the bar a stunned silence, like a Mexican Wave, followed him, and as he minced past me the reason was obvious. Like the rest of his cronies he was all in leather – no problem – 'butt' no arse! Well he had an arse, just a very bare hairy one! Oh my God! You could hardly hear the jukebox for the sound of closet doors slamming. He caused an uproar. But there was an ugly murmur. Trouble was brewing and brewing fast. I had to act quickly.

Not only a Mexican Wave, but a Mexican stand-off. Perm, all five feet of him, was facing up to the biggest, meanest homophobic thug in town. He was going to be murdered. But I hadn't counted on the rest of the girls. First on the scene was Tina the Tranny, backed by Clipper and, forgive the pun, bringing up the rear was Tint himself.

Now they were all exponents of the art of Kick Boxing. Some could kick and some could box, but all could fight. I mean they could *really* fight and God help the fucker who got blood on Tint's jumpsuit.

It was all over in couple of minutes. Three poofs and a pseudo tranny had demolished the town's best and were off to do more damage elsewhere.

As for us, we were left with lots more arses!

# Hair today ... gone tomorrow

Now, I am the customer from hell: I have seen more hairdressers off than a bad case of alopecia. I am a nightmare. But I don't care what it costs and I am the best tipper around. However, woe betide the hairdresser who takes one centimetre more off the length than I have specified. I had been using the same girl for years and could not believe she would have the audacity to get pregnant.

For some time Tint had been trying to woo me to his salon but I had steadfastly refused until now. I had seen no reason to spoil a good friendship but there seemed to be no alternative and after all, they were good customers. Maybe it was time for pay back. I duly made my appointment and the evening before I was due to be 'done' we had a pow wow to make sure everything would go to plan.

First: no cutting off more than I wanted. Agreed. The very lightest of perm lotions, just to give body. Agreed. No leaving me to nip next door. Agreed. Things should have been fine but deep in my heart I knew it was all going to go wrong and they'd be customers no more.

The fateful day dawned and in I tripped. I was treated like royalty and had a squad of apprentices falling over themselves to take my coat (I only lived next door), get me coffee, a magazine and every other service the salon offered. The great man arrived. Now Tint very seldom attended to clients personally and maybe I should have taken that as a hint!

I was given the full consultation, obviously what we'd agreed the night before had gone by the by. Or was it the three bottles of wine consumed whilst debating the issue? Anyway, we went through the whole procedure once again.

Off I was whisked to be prepped. I was subjected to a full body massage but only on my head! And it took fully fifteen minutes to shampoo and whatever else. Then the fiasco began.

I had instructed them that I wanted the perm completed first and then the cut the reason being, every hairdresser cuts and then when your hair is permed, it is shorter by another inch. But no, no, they knew best. As the perm was developing my hair looked as if it was lighter than before and I called one of them over to check.

"No, no everything's fine." The lotion was washed off and it was immediately obvious that my hair was definitely lighter; a sort of gingerish colour. Now came the cut. Only the ends, remember, only the ends. Well, they did cut only the ends, over and over again. But the best was yet to come.

Whilst I was being shampooed the next client had arrived and was in the chair next to me, sharing a mirror. Lo and behold! The wife of the publican I most detested.

"Interesting," was all she said.

I looked in the mirror and fuck me! I looked like a cross between a poodle and Crystal Tips with her hand in a socket. My head was one huge triangular frizz of ginger hair!

"Don't worry, don't worry it'll be fine."

Well, the more they did the less fine it became. It ended up looking like an unravelled Brillo pad and I was apoplectic!

It took six months and three other hairdressers for me to lift the ban on them.

# The Vat Man

Over the years I had a few VAT inspections. The first was a brief cursory examination, I was fined a few quid but nothing much. However, the next two were far more frightening and thorough, and coincidentally, were handled by the same officer: Mr. Black from Fife.

Mr. Black arrived one winter's morning by appointment, along with my accountant. He was a dour-looking individual and looked like he could do with a good feed. I have to say I was absolutely terrified of what he was going to find (honest person that I am) but everyone fiddles the VAT at some time. I was appalled at the thought of jail but believe me, it was a distinct possibility.

Now John, my accountant, is without doubt the most boring man I have ever met in my life. However, it is all an act; he has perfected this gift of simply talking and talking and talking in the most monotonous way, but he is such a nice and helpful man no one actually wants to cut him to the quick.

Within the first hour we had discovered Mr. Black had two kids, had been in the Revenue for all his working life and he had Crohn's disease and quite simply he hated his job, and wanted to retire on grounds of ill health.

We made all the right noises, made him comfortable and promised to make life as easy as possible. For some unholy reason this worked. He was obviously made to feel as uncomfortable as possible on other premises and I can understand why. But he almost became my very BFF.

A VAT inspection on premises like mine can take months so we were in it for the long haul. On days when I knew he was coming I had the fire in the bar lit early so the room was comfortable. We made him coffee and a small breakfast. John spent as long as he could chatting so that most of the morning was taken up in pleasantries. We let him do a bit of work then it was lunch time and he had delicious homemade soup and tit-bits.

One of the symptoms of Crohn's disease is that you spend an awful lot of time in toilets and usually they are very public or not particularly pleasant. So here he was: private suite, warm surroundings, food and coffee on tap.

In the afternoon he did a bit of work, and then into the car and off home around 3pm to miss the traffic. All in all, he really didn't get much done and John and I knew he would have limited time to wrap up the case.

During the time he was with us, we fed him and

cosseted him and I have to say it paid off. Of course he found anomalies but he kept it to the minimum. He had to be seen to be doing his job but we got off more than lightly and we parted on excellent terms, hoping never to see one another again professionally.

Over the next few years Mr and Mrs. Black and the Black children visited us from time to time and of course were extended my hospitality; they never abused it and of course, I was earning Brownie points. Points I never thought I'd ever need to cash in!

On the very day I sold the pub, unbelievably, an appointment for an inspection arrived. Well, I thought I was high and dry, but oh no! Even though I wouldn't be in residence, the business was still functioning and had not been wound up. An inspection had been arranged and an inspection would be carried out. I was gutted; let's face it I would never be that lucky again, or would I?

On the morning of the first visit I was in John's office and believe me, I was bricking it. Lo and behold, who turned up but Mr. Black and he was delighted to see us. Greeted me like a long lost pal and spent the whole morning in John's office reminiscing. Yes his kids were doing well and yes he still hated his job and his Crohn's disease was getting worse. What a shame we had sold up, he had really been looking forward to spending time there. Apparently he had volunteered for the job!

We spent all the morning chatting and I don't think

any work was done, but as he was preparing to leave, he said a very strange thing. He assured me that he hadn't cost me much money the last time and he didn't expect it would be much this time. That was all very well; you'd think I would have learned my lesson. Oh fuck! I'd fiddled treble the amount this time and the prospect of jail was looming large again.

He settled into a routine very quickly. He'd come on Tuesday and Friday and in between we'd produce the fictitious figures he was looking for. John and I met on Monday and Thursday to get everything right.

Towards the conclusion of the case I arrived at John's office one Monday morning as usual and was astounded to find the alarm activated and three squad cars in attendance.

John arrived and on entering the building, who did we find but a very red faced Mr. Black? His 9am appointment had failed to turn up and having nothing particular to do and not wanting to return to his office, he had decided to call on John for a cup of coffee and a catch-up.

Arriving at the office, he had found it open but no John, who he assumed would be on his way. Due to over-indulgence at the weekend his illness had been playing up and he had retired to the loo with his paper, delighted to have the place to himself. In the meantime, the other inhabitant of the building had had to leave, checked that there was no-one in any of the other offices, locked up, set the alarm and headed off.

Meantime, Mr. Black had enjoyed the solitude, finished his paper and ablutions and prepared to face the day again. As soon as he left the comfort and safety of the toilet of course, all the alarms were activated and he couldn't vacate the premises as they were locked from the outside. He would have to explain to his superiors what he was doing on the other side of town when he should have been working on another case.

As you can guess, not a story he would want to get out. He wrapped up my case there and then, and in fact I got a small rebate.

# Tweety pie . . .

As a publican you are expected to know everything. What time the chemist closes? Where's the nearest bank? Often the requests to do or keep things border on the ridiculous.

One afternoon one of the 'smelly brigade' asked the barmaid to put a small box behind the bar for safety. It was a small white box with what looked to be air holes along the side. Now and again there was a slight scratching sound coming from it. Lisa the barmaid was too busy to pay attention or investigate.

Then enters the landlord: my husband. Now David has a 'thing' about 'things' behind the bar; he goes mad, and quite rightly too. Drinks are being served and can be contaminated so unidentified 'things' should not be there.

Of course, what's the first thing he spies? The box.

"What's this?" He roars, picking it up and shaking it extremely violently.

"Hey, what you doin' with ma budgie?" shouts the owner of the box.

Oh dear! I hope it wasn't the last one in the shop!

# Lost property . . .

Jackets, coats, umbrellas, mobile phones and shopping were all left with such regularity that we stopped even having a Lost Property – the building wasn't big enough. One lady phoned, asking if we had found her dentures. Items like these are left so frequently we actually tape them together and date them. What happens is; the diner orders a steak, finds he or she can't chew it, takes out their teeth and wraps them in a napkin. Yes, they forget and then throw the napkin away. So when the girls are clearing tables they will always shake the napkin just in case.

Anyway, this lady phoned to ask if we had come across her dentures. The form of identification is the date; that narrows it down a bit. She informed us her party were in the Carvery on Boxing Day. Nothing strange about that? It was now the 12th of March. Obviously she didn't go out much!

I've had a glass eye and a false leg left, not by the same person. Well I don't think so. I mean how can people forget such things? An umbrella I can understand. Jackets, yes. Mobile phones, yes. But a fucking false leg?  Surely you'd wonder why you were walking in circles, or hopping!  I can't 'see' how anyone wouldn't miss a glass eye, but they did and it was never claimed.

Babies; you wouldn't believe how many babies! Mother comes in, meets her cronies, has a few spritzers and then goes off merrily, leaving the baby in our care. Fantastic!  Just what we want, a shitty, smelly, crying baby.

# The Grafter

I used to dread Monday mornings, or 'Giro Days' as we called them. Oh, we were busy enough but the bar resembled a doctor's surgery or, as Zander used to call it, 'God's waiting room'. This is where we were entertaining the walking wounded. Such a collection of walking sticks, zimmer frames, neck braces, plaster casts, aka 'stookies' was incredible. And that was just the staff!

Most of my allegedly disabled regulars were fitter and more agile than I, but I was expected to work a twelve hour day to cater for them and listen to their grouches and arguments as to whose condition was the worst. Unbelievably this often resulted in ridiculous challenges and Herculean tasks. That is, until they remembered they were 'disabled' and would lose their money!

There was one who actually ended up in the News of the World branded as a benefit cheat. Norman was a scallywag; you know the type: not really bad but as fly as the devil. He had a squad of kids and his wife had gone off on the trot with some toy boy or other and left Norman literally holding the baby. All seven of them!

He was a grafter and had run his own building business for years. Not quite a cowboy, more an Indian, but a cheap one at that. He drove a reasonably nice car and was never short of money. He looked after all his kids and looked after them well. All in all, he was reckoned to be one of the good guys! The men he would employ from time to time always spoke well of him and they never had to go looking for their money.

No wonder! This bugger, it seems, knew every dodge in the book. And every benefit that could be claimed would be claimed by him. He was entitled to God knows how much Family Allowance (seven kids) Family Income Support; one of the children needed extra support so there was an allowance for that.

He was claiming Invalidity Allowance (bad back) Attendance Allowance (even sorer back) Mobility Allowance (nice car!) and every other government run scheme available. This went on for years and he had an income of about £25K in benefits alone. Being a successful builder would bring its rewards too and it was estimated that he was earning £60K to £70K tax free. Not bad for someone with a bad back!

The main problem with being a cheat is that you can't afford to upset anyone and to be fair, Norman was a nice guy and it wasn't really a problem he'd encountered before. But now there was the ex-wife.

It appeared that, having tired of the magnificent sex with the toy boy, she wasn't as young as she made out to be and she hankered after her old life. Norman was nothing if not generous (let's face it he could afford to be!) But he was having none of it. She'd made her bed and could lie in it for a while longer as far as he was concerned. Woe betide him. 'Hell Hath No Fury' and of course she knew all his little secrets (not that little!) because she'd devised most of them.

Norman had worked away steadily for years and years. He was maybe a little complacent and did not for one moment think anyone would be watching him or investigating his ten year benefit claim. It is likely that this would have gone on for another ten years if only he'd forgiven his wife!

She was a vicious little monkey and despite having produced seven mini Normans (all boys) she had managed to keep her looks and appearance but at quite a cost. A cost she could no longer afford. The toy boy certainly could not support her on his paper round and pocket money. So she was pressurizing Norman for some dosh. He really was a canny bloke; she had humiliated him and he knew it was only the money she was after. He was adamant she wasn't getting any! Big mistake!

After threats, promises and pleading she realised it was a no go. So despite professing her undying love for him and the kids, she promptly went off to the DHSS and shopped him. But that wasn't enough for

Mrs. Norman! Straight off to the Sunday papers and a nice little earner. Think about it, £25K for at least ten years, that was a big story.

The following week, emblazoned across the front page of the Sunday papers was a picture of Norman carrying not one, not two but three huge bags of cement and the headline was 'Cheating Chancer Cons Benefits Office.' Just think what he could have carried if his back had been okay.

He was done for! He lost all his extras and nearly landed in jail. Strangely enough though, he became this sort of Robin Hood figure in the town. Everyone felt sorry for him and didn't blame him in the least. The consensus of opinion was, rightly or wrongly, if you can get away with it, good for you. And let's face it, with seven kids he'd need all that money.

He still drives a nice car . . .

# DRINKING VOCABULARY
## CHALLENGE

Things that are difficult to say when you're drunk . . .

- Innovative
- Preliminary
- Proliferation
- Cinnamon

Things that are *VERY* difficult to say when you're drunk . . .

- Specificity
- British Constitution
- Passive-aggressive disorder
- Transubstantiate

Things that are *ABSOLUTELY IMPOSSIBLE* to say when you're drunk . . .

- Thanks, but I don't want to sleep with you.
- Nope, no more booze for me.
- Sorry, but you're not really my type.
- No kebab for me, thank you.
- Good evening officer, isn't it lovely out tonight? I'm not interested in fighting you.
- Oh, I just couldn't - no one wants to hear me sing.
- Thanks but no I won't make any attempt to dance, I have no co-ordination. I'd hate to look like a fool.
- Where is the nearest toilet? I refuse to vomit in the street.
- I must be going home now as I have work in the morning

# Everyone's a winner

Racing is an integral part of our town and the racing fraternity are big business. Staff and owners from all the racing stables throughout the country will at some point arrive in Edinburgh.

Most of the pubs in town have a band of regulars, punters as well as participants, and each meeting was looked forward to with great anticipation.

Because we were 'the place to eat' we were fortunate that we attracted customers from all sectors. Most of the owners and trainers and at some point all of the travelling lads came through. Now the travelling lads, especially the head lads, were the ones to cultivate. They knew, before they started the engine on the horse box, which horse was going to win or had a damn good chance. Over the years we had had a few good tips and of course a few 'dead certs'. But there is one occasion which will go down in history.

Quite often trainers in Newmarket or Ascot will send horses to a small course like ours to try them out. As you can appreciate, this is enormously costly and often they will share the costs with a couple of other stables. Most race-goers know that these horses are certainly not 'sure things'. However, when a trainer accompanies the horse, together with travelling staff of at least three others then that horse has a chance.

Towards the end of the flat season, a Monday meeting was scheduled which was great for business. The race-goers all arrived early Sunday and once their charges were attended to, they went out to play. These guys could play and one stable in particular were great favourites of ours. The head lad (bit of a misnomer, he was pushing sixty) was a hard drinker and one of the few who never gave out racing tips but he was great fun and a great tipper. The staff all loved him and I think because we didn't pester him, he felt at ease.

This particular visit, he had arrived with a bunch of his cronies and they were roaring drunk. For a couple of hours they argued and bickered about whose horse was best and whose would win and so on and so forth. Just at closing time while waiting for his taxi, he sidled up to me and whispered, 'Put your shirt on ***'. He was so drunk and his thick Irish accent meant I couldn't make out what he was saying.

Normally I would let it go but this was so out the ordinary I was intrigued. I went off looking for his understudies and told them what he had said. They were gobsmacked, as they were always under strict orders to keep shtum! The lads don't get paid much and one way to boost their income is a few tips here and there. This lot were never allowed that luxury.

So when they knew the Boss had given me info, they knew it was good. It appeared they had brought a newbie up from Newmarket called LA Colt. It had never run before and the odds were huge.

The next morning at breakfast, the staff were talking about the race meeting and I told them about the conversation. I sent the KP over to the bookies to find out what the odds were on this horse and when it came back as 100/1, I literally pooh-poohed it. But the rest were adamant they would have a flutter.

Everyone round the breakfast table put their stake into the pot and just as I was counting up, a customer who had borrowed £20 the night before came to pay it back. Oh well! Must be fate; tenner each way for me. I must say, I am not and never have been a gambler, but this seemed too good to miss.

Off I went to pace the bet. The bookie, who was a customer of mine, jokingly commented he was getting some of his money back. This horse had no chance; you know all the usual quips. The only thing I had been told to do was make sure we got the 'first show price'. This meant nothing to me but I did what I was told.

It was an extremely busy shift and to be honest, I don't think anyone gave the bet another thought till the race was well over. While we were enjoying our coffee, we sent the KP back across to find out if we had won anything. Thinking even if it came in fourth we'd get something back.

The fucking beauty had only won! Yes, it had won and we scooped nearly six grand between us. It was certainly party night that night, and boy did we party! It felt like we'd won the lottery. It was months before anyone from that stable passed through but you can be assured they were well taken care of.

As for the head lad, he never got that drunk again, well not in my pub. And as for the bookie, well! Every time he saw me enter the premises (not often) he went a deathly shade of pale.

# It could be you . . .

I have known a number of Lottery winners; some have won real big and others a tidy sum. One of these happened on a Saturday night in November. One of my customers, a nice chap, called Charles, came in every Saturday night around ten along with his sister, and her pal who worked for me. They had been doing this for years. All were married but their partners either didn't drink or had other hobbies.

This particular Saturday was really busy and we got a call from Charles' wife, asking that he phone her. OK, no problem, but she phoned and phoned and phoned.

Now you can't believe how irritating this is on any night. But Saturday is impossible. You are screaming down the phone because the bar is so noisy, you seldom get the right name and you forget the message. This night she kept phoning every ten minutes or so and she said something about winning?

Now as it happened, he and the girls, were later than usual. Maybe this is what she was on about. One of them had won a few quid at the bingo and they'd stayed for another drink. I have to say I didn't think it merited all this attention.

Because there had been so many calls, we pulled the plug out on the phone and, strange though it seems having had so many calls, we all forgot to tell him.

Just before closing I suddenly remembered. Christ! Hoping it wasn't something serious I bawled across the bar to him that he had to call his wife. Bloody hell! He had twenty missed calls and he was in a state. Something awful must have happened.

Well, something had happened but not something awful. His wife had checked his lottery ticket and he'd only won £90K! Now he wanted to buy everyone in the bar a drink. But fuck! The last bell had gone . . . it was too late.

I had missed my chance to help him celebrate but hey ho. Although I didn't get any of his winnings that night, I got more than my share over the next few weeks!

# Customers Wanted

On taking over Tweedy's way back in the very early 90's I wanted to let people know we had arrived, and to attract not only more, but a different class of customer. Not the usual 'Under New Management' banner for me. This, in my opinion, just attracted the idiots that the previous owners had barred. We had to do something different! But what?

Tweedy's was a fairly run down pub with fairly run down customers. It was full of ne'er-do-wells who were mostly barred from all the other watering holes in town. It was unaffectionately known as 'Cardboard City' and on our first morning I was aghast at the ragbag of people looking back at me over the bar.

Although this was my home town, I had been away for a long time and wasn't really known. I, on the other hand, knew everyone. Well, here goes I thought. I smiled broadly and offered them all a complimentary drink. By the looks on their faces, they thought their birthdays and Christmases had come at once. Each one of them was calculating what they could take this mug for!

I politely asked if they had enjoyed my hospitality while removing all the glasses from the bar. It was obvious that most thought a refill was on its way! But no! I informed them that I hoped they had enjoyed their drinks because it would be their last on these premises while I was in residence. There and then I barred twenty seven people, virtually the whole customer base. Oh my God . . . had I thrown the baby out with the bathwater?

For the first few weeks we could count the customers on one hand. Had I gone too far? Whatever. It was too late now!

Time for action, what was I going to do? We were losing money hand over fist and I had to come up with something! I drew up a list of all the qualities we would want in the 'perfect customer" but how to get to them, or attract them, was the problem. How did other businesses get their customers? That was when I came up with the novel idea of advertising for customers.

Now, our local paper was unwilling at first to run such a unique offer. It was not, in their opinion, a bona fide position. But with a bit of cajoling and some moral blackmail, they eventually succumbed.

The advertisement appeared the following Friday in the Situations Vacant section and had a very mixed reception. I had numerous daft beggars actually ring for an interview! Had a couple of people who took real exception to it and accused me of making a mockery of the unemployment situation. But the majority thought it was funny and came along to see us. That was not the end of it!

The following week we were besieged by the national newspapers who portrayed me as a real idiot who had bought this bar, found we had no customers and had resorted to desperate measures! I appeared on Scotland Today, again, as some poor fool who had sold a pub in the poorest area of Scotland to come to an even poorer one.

People were pouring in. I could not have bought this amount of publicity. It was fantastic, and quite frankly they could make me out to be the biggest fool in Christendom as long as we achieved the desired effect.

Because of its success and the huge increase in custom, we carried out a major refurbishment and on reopening, had 500 tee shirts printed with the slogan . . .

**Tweedy Customer,
I got the Job.**

Not bad for a fool!

# CUSTOMERS WANTED

Due to the recent change of ownership and
the downturn in the economic climate we
will be interviewing for new customers
at Tweedy's Bar on Monday 26th July.  To
qualify for the position, the following
criteria must be met:

Must be minimum 18 years old

Sound financial status

Available between 11am - 11pm weekdays
and

11am - 1am weekends

Pleasant disposition.

No experience required – training will be
given

Apply in Person to the above address.

Patrons previously barred need not apply.

# 118 118

Often you'd get involved in the daftest of conversations and not have a clue how, or what the hell it was about. Worse than that, you are sober but sound like the stupid one.

Two dafties who came in every day were obsessed with the bus and train schedules. They continually asked me: what time was the next bus? What about the one after and which one went where? What about trains? When was the next one? What time would it arrive? What infuriated me was the daft buggers lived nowhere near a train station and would have to catch a bus from the station home. So the next question would be about the buses running from the station. It drove me mad!

For example:"Will the number 44 take me to Haddington?" asks one.

"Noooo . . . 'fraid not," I reply.

"What about me?" asks the other daftie . . .

# The Sober Man's Visit to the Bathroom:

1. Walk determinedly up to the bathroom, make sure everyone knows that is where you are headed.
2. Enter the bathroom and quickly check it out.
3. Look for the right urinal. Which is the right one? Well there must be at least one empty one between you and the next person (preferably on either side). If this is not possible, take the one next to the wall, beside a "safe-looking" male. If this is also not possible, leave and return later.
4. If the required urinal is available then approach it swiftly looking straight ahead, no eye contact.
5. Undo trousers, relieve yourself as quickly as possible, keeping your head down (or eyes closed and head held up). This way no-one will think you are checking them out.
6. Shake it off and put it away.
7. Wash hands.
8. Attempt to dry hands. Look to see if a blow

dryer or paper towel dispenser is close by. If not, your clothes will do just fine.

9. Exit bathroom, do NOT look back, you didn't forget anything.

10. Check to see if your female companion has exited the bathroom before you, although highly unlikely, you must check anyway.

11. Wait patiently for her return, remember NOT to say anything like "What the fuck took you so long?"

# . . . And a visit to the Ladies

1. Enter bathroom, checking each cubicle, but NOT the first one. The first one is bad luck. Look to see what stall is the nicest looking and has plenty of toilet paper.
2. Damn! The bitch who came in just behind you has bagged it.
3. Curse under your breath and make a dash for second choice, in case skanky trollop coming in will get it.
4. Hang jacket and handbag on hook provided.
5. Take handfuls of toilet paper and wipe the seat, making sure you wipe off all the germs.
6. Line toilet seat with toilet paper. Germs are bad.
7. Start to take off all layers of required clothing, ensuring nothing touches the ground.
8. Preferably squat or hover over the toilet seat but, if absolutely necessary, sit very lightly so as not to disturb the layer of paper between you and the seat. Germs are bad.
9. Now go, making sure you are still hovering or

sitting lightly, because the paper on the seat
MUST NOT move or you'll get germs.

10. Peel off at least 29 sheets of toilet paper from
the roll. Fold into a neat rectangle and wipe
all drips very carefully. Do not get germs
from the seat.

11. Put back on the 14 layers of clothing you
were wearing. Make sure you look exactly
like you did when you first entered.

12. Put all toilet paper that was lining the seat
into toilet and flush at least twice.

13. Exit cubicle and make for the cleanest sink.

14. Put hands under running water for at least two
minutes.

15. Lather up with lots of soap, get everywhere
exposed to germs.

16. Rinse soap off hands under water for another
two minutes.

17. Check for paper towels or stick hands under
blow dryer for four minutes – NEVER WIPE
HANDS ON CLOTHING!

18. Spread out contents of bag on counter.

19. Touch up already perfect make-up. This
should take no longer than five to ten minutes.

20. Return all contents to bag.

21. Exit powder room.

22. Find boyfriend outside. Wonder how he gets
done so fast . . . You were really quick this
time.

# In the Sh*t . . .

The unsung heroes in any licensed establishment are the girls, not the sexy barmaids (of course they are important). Not the cordon bleu chef. Not the cellar man and certainly not the landlady. Who are these girls?

They are the cleaners of course, without whom the poor landlord/lady would have to rise at some ungodly hour, probably only two hours after they had gone to bed to deal with the disgusting human remains from the night before.

These girls are a breed unto themselves and mine were in a class of their own. Heather and Maisie were with me for fifteen years, during which time they dealt with more unmentionables than can be mentioned. Maisie was in her seventies when we inherited her and was a wonderful hard-working lady to whom nothing was a problem. She sung (out of tune) constantly and no matter what she encountered, she dealt with it. Her partner on the other hand was a one-off. I had never before met anyone like Heather and I know I never will again.

She was small, wiry and as hard as nails, had a PhD in swearing and about as ladylike as a squad of Irish navvies. But she was fiercely loyal, reliable, and honest to the core and could do the work of four.

The girls arrived at half seven on the dot every morning, with the exception of Christmas Day and New Year's Day. The state of the premises, especially the gent's toilets could be gauged by Heather's "fuck O meter".

What is a "fuck O meter" and how does it work? Well no other pub to the best of my knowledge has one, because no other pub has a Heather. And how does this "fuck O meter" work?

Well on their arrival on a fairly typical weekday morning the average amount of garbage and toilet debris was met with "F. . .U. . .C. . .K. . .I. . .N' H. . .E. . .L. . .L. . .!!!! Roared at the top of her voice and could be heard up to three streets away. This was the usual gentle introduction to the day for me.

A busy Friday or Saturday was anything from:

"FUCKING DIRTY B ****** S" to "I'LL STRING THE C***S UP BY THEIR BALLS".

This could be heard in the next town and was so scary even the cat took cover. Me? I dived back under the duvet and no way would I appear till the worst was over.

But the really frightening scenario was when nothing could be heard. No Fucking Hell. No Dirty B*****ds. No C***s. Just a low guttural groan would emit from her and you knew that what was being said under her breath could never be seen in print. In fact, even she couldn't say it out loud. Her face would turn a peculiar shade of puce and she would throw so many gallons of bleached water around the toilets looked like the bridge of the Titanic.

The Gent's is the one place a pub cleaner dreads; mind you the Ladies isn't a walk in the park, but in general is not as malodorous as the other. The disgusting habits of the male populace is absolutely unbelievable and I've been so embarrassed and guilty at what I was asking the girls to deal with that I've paid them double, and in some monumental cases, triple time.

After even the quietest of sessions when there have been only a handful of customers, it still looks like a troop of incontinent monkeys has been on the rampage. I'm convinced that most visitors simply open the door and let go.

Heather's theory was that a man's penis (I won't say what she called it!) has a mind of its own. He can go into the loo, take perfect aim and yet still manage to piss all over the toilet tissue, down his trouser leg and over his shoes. This when he is relatively sober, you don't want to imagine what happens after ten pints.

Sometimes a lad would go into the facilities and take aim, but because no-one was watching he'd try to beat the record of "how high". Or if really bored would just begin spinning round and round or back and forth imitating his garden hose, spraying everything. The light fitting, the dryers, soap dispenser, even other visitors if he got too carried away.

You don't believe me? Ask any man.

Countless numbers of soiled boxers and Y-fronts are left in the cistern on Friday and Saturday nights and many a relationship has broken up because her man returned home minus his kecks, and rather than admit to being caught short and dumping the offending garments in our cistern, endured the ignominy of being battered senseless, or in some extreme cases thrown out.

So many were there that the staff could tell from experience which ones were now going commando and we even took bets on it. How did we prove it? Trade secret!

One customer, who shall remain nameless, had the nerve to apologise to the cleaners for a little mishap. He had been suffering for a few days with constipation and to relieve his symptoms his wife had given him a dose of Epsom Salts. That, coupled with five pints of Guinness, had done the trick. But he had unfortunately been unable to wait until he reached the comfort of his own little room and been forced to use ours. On hearing this Heather was absolutely incensed, bearing in mind she had first-hand experience of his little problem. She roared at him in front of all his mates

"Fucking salts! Epsom Fucking Salts! Listen pal, whatever it was you took, there was no need to do fucking somersaults!" and stormed off. The poor soul was mortified and was known for ever after as the Needle (shit through the eye of).

It's always the most macho of men who turn who turn out to be the biggest wimps. A prime example was big Jim. This lad was a six foot three, eighteen stone, beer-swilling rugby player who swaggered about playing the hard man most Friday nights. You know the type, the one who would definitely kick sand in your face. But the cleaners were his "Waterloo".

On a particularly nasty Saturday morning, Heather and Maisie set about cleaning the gents and clearing out all the unwanted gifts. Normally everything is picked up and disposed of without anything but a cursory glance. Let's face it, would you want to examine a pair of skanky boxers covered in unmentionable bodily fluids? No? Well neither did they. However, just as one stinking piece was about to disappear into the nether regions of the bin, Heather noticed a name tag stitched into the waist band. Now the pants had to be years old as the name tag was so faded that it had to have been sewn on in case the owner lost or misplaced them at Scout Camp! Unfortunately for the owner of these pants, the name was still legible. I knew she wouldn't let him off lightly under these circumstances. Jim, being such an arse, was going to be crucified, with my blessing.

The offending garment was doubly wrapped to contain the germ-ridden fabric, not to mention the smell, and then beautifully gift-wrapped, ready to present to him.

Heather and a couple of the barmaids set the trap and convinced most of the customers that he had won first prize in a raffle. In he came, strutting about as usual like "cock of the walk" and when it was announced that he had won a prize, up he came like a lamb to the slaughter. So eager was he to see his prize that he ripped off the paper, including the plastic there and then. It took him a few minutes to realize what the sodden stinking mess was. By which time the whole pub was in an uproar.

Talk yourself out of that one big man!

# Monday Club

Many hostelries throughout the country have a Monday club. An unofficial holiday from work and, or, either the recovery of, or the continuation of the weekend.

For the publican, it can be the most lucrative session of the week. A Monday club cannot be manufactured; it evolves and exists by tradition. Only certain pubs have the "X" factor which allows a Monday club. Its members come from all over town and very often do not regularly drink in this particular watering-hole. It is not unusual to see bitter rivals, who would normally be at each other's throats, drinking side-by-side

Entrance to the club is open to anyone and it consists of hard-core diehards who would only miss Mondays if hospitalized, dead or at Her Majesty's pleasure. These members are seldom in gainful employment and normally rely on the receipt of their Giro, Monday book or Child Allowance and range in age from eighteen to 'check for a pulse'.

The Associate members are in the main, feckless individuals who attend for a variety of reasons but the most popular being:

"Having an absolute fucker of a hangover!"

*or*
"Been kicked out by the wife/girlfriend!"

*perhaps*
"Been sacked for turning up to work still drunk!"

*often*
"Just been released from police cells!"

*sometimes*
"Their mates dragged them in!"

*simply*
"Don't want the weekend to end!"

Whatever the reason these creatures attend with regularity but not with the absolute tenacity of a diehard

Our hard-core was made up of the two sets of twins, the smelly brigade, Bob the builder and whoever he was working with that week; Mondays being against his particular religion. The lone stranger (wait till you hear his story!) Almost every chef in town – God help anyone who was feeling peckish – no chance! We always had a couple of grave diggers in attendance. We could never understand who dug the graves for the dear-departed whose misfortune it was to be buried on

201

a Monday; a mystery never solved. But they seldom, if ever, missed the club. The one-armed bandit, a bloody nuisance at any time but particularly bad on Mondays. Then there was desperate Anne and a seventy year old drag queen, old Dolly. My theory is he wasn't actually a drag queen just a dirty old sod who had run out of clean clothes of his own and had started on his dead wife's.

Are you getting the picture? An extremely busy bar with the most bizarre collection of drink-sodden, pee-stained, minging customers and for the next five to six hours they were all mine. Oh! Lucky me!

The associate members would begin to arrive any time after nine in the morning. They would come sidling in by the side door desperately in need of "a hair of the dog". There was an element of shame being seen entering licensed premises this early but most were simply terrified their mother or other half would catch them. Shame didn't come into it.

The diehards would drift in nearer to the official opening time of eleven, having partaken of a light breakfast; a can of Super Lager and ten fags, collected their Giro or whatever H.M. Government bonus scheme they happened to have qualified for and which provided their beer vouchers for the day, and made their leisurely way to the pub, via the newsagent and the bookies.

By now the place was usually standing room only, but incredibly hushed. This was most unusual for a packed bar. Remember however, most of these guys were nursing the devil of all hangovers, many having to drink through a straw to avoid spillage and certainly not fit to conduct an intellectual conversation about "whether the landlord had cleaned his pipes or not" or any debate for that matter about his internal plumbing.

This gentle introduction to the day was sacrosanct and anyone breaching the rules was dealt with swiftly. Most were just turfed out, but a few were knocked out, depending on who they had disturbed. This cathedral-like reverence lasted usually until the third or fourth drink had been consumed and the gentle hum of intellectual banter such as "Who the fuck drank ma' pint?" Or "What are you looking at ya bam?" had risen to cacophonous, deafening proportions.

The party had started and it was bring on the dancing girls. Unfortunately we were often quite short on the dancing girl front, so we had to rely on two toothless hags from the Nag's Head who were constantly pissed to the eyeballs and fancied themselves as pole dancers. No-one else fancied them, well not yet anyway! Think beer-goggles. The fact that we had no pole spoke volumes about the state of their audience.

Club membership was certainly not exclusive although prospective candidates had to meet certain criteria.

First and foremost you had to be a drunk, or certainly have the makings of one.

You had to be able to hold down a reasonable

quantity of drink. Short-timers were no good to the landlord or the patrons – took up valuable space

You had to have sufficient funds from whatever source to finance your membership.

It also helped if you were a bit of an imbecile, fully-fledged morons always welcomed, but the gold card-holders were the complete arseholes, who usually had fast track passes to both A & E and the local constabulary.

The club agenda also followed a strict format. It was always quiet to begin with; this eases the members into action. Then three or four hours of frenetic partying and the last hour is time to settle up, and not always the bill.

All members took part in some form of entertainment. The main turn is the beloved karaoke. The Japanese have been responsible for more murders by karaoke than by kamikaze. Of course believing you could be the re-incarnation of Elvis wasn't to everyone's taste. There was the card school, killer pool (and it often came near to). Or, maybe just plain boring the arse off anyone within earshot and believe me there was no shortage of talent.

Always first on stage was desperate Ann. At first glance Ann appeared to be an upright citizen, who resembled the quintessential Presbyterian Sunday School teacher until she downed her first super lager. After which, it was goodbye Sunday school and hello cougar. Anne was a cougar before the world knew what the expression meant. In our day she was simply a slapper.

It was rumoured she held down an extremely high-powered job in local government but however she managed it, she never worked on Mondays and therefore qualified as an honorary member.

No man was safe from Anne (hence the "desperate"). Her only criteria was that her target had to have a pulse. She was on the prowl constantly and had been caught in more compromising situations than Monica Lewinsky. Over the years she had been battered by wives, girlfriends and even the odd boyfriend but this never deterred her. She was a menace and sex mad. It made no difference if her intended victim was with his partner; she simply ignored them and moved in. It was so blatant that most of the women couldn't believe their eyes. But as she persevered with her capture, the end result was often a cat-fight and she seldom came out on top.

She was lethal on the mike, firstly, she had a voice like a navvy; she danced like a navvy, and trying to retrieve the mike took a squad of navvies.

Desperate Anne was usually followed by big Agnes, wife of the local fishmonger. Remember, nothing should smell of fish except fish. Her weekly rendition of *Big Spender* was legend, but her pelvic thrust when popping her cork invariably knocked out half the audience especially the uninitiated associate members. She dressed in a style all her own and her hair appeared to have been neither washed nor combed since the sixties, not her sixties but the nineteen sixties. Never one to miss a business opportunity she always carried a bit of stock about her person, which added to the aroma.

Agnes's beleaguered husband, wee Eck, couldn't sing, dance nor recite poetry. That didn't stop him for one moment. His party piece was–apart from smelling even worse than his wife–*My Way*. It was the nearest he ever got to getting his way as she definitely wore the trousers. Just a shame they were always two sizes too small.

While the karaoke drowned out most of the other conversations and activities it never interfered with the card school. A friendly game; where no money was ever to change hands. But it was amazing how many fights broke out over a couple of match sticks.

One stalwart of the card school was big Stevie the window cleaner. It was a standing joke amongst all the regulars that he was the only window cleaner who didn't do house calls.

Week in and week out Stevie would arrive in great fettle and full of optimism. He was going to take them all to the cleaners. He talked a big game, pity he couldn't play one.

Stevie had a "system". The fact that he consistently lost and lost big would have alerted anyone else to the fact that the system wasn't working, but not him.

Of course, the other players encouraged him as

they systematically relieved him of his wad week after week.

Without fail Stevie left each week, pot-less and saying that he couldn't beat a lucky player. He couldn't understand why he never got that lucky streak. It never dawned on him that he just couldn't play and no-one was likely to put him wise to this fact because they were all making money off him.

Over the course of the eight to ten hours of the Monday club there was an amazing maelstrom of movement. There was constant to-ing and fro-ing across to the bookies. Bodies in and out to the cashpoints, for obvious reasons. Wives hunting down lost husbands, dumping screaming children. Husbands too inebriated to recognise their own kids and generously offering to buy them a pint or maybe a whisky chaser. I'd bloody chase them if any belonged to me. We had loan sharks and landlords looking for payment from errant debtors and many a patron skipped out the back door undetected with our assistance. If anyone was going to relieve them of their pennies it was going to be us!

There were occasional trips to the local chippie. Boozers have to eat once in a while and there would be little or no sustenance at home after their escapades and many a body propelled through the door for a variety of reasons

It was normally about two-ish when the snarling began and those fucking twins were always in at the start. They were inveterate gamblers and whilst

Harry was ensconced in the poker game, Gerry, the non-stutterer would bounce back and forth to the bookies. Constantly interrupting the game by seeking his brother's advice, or imparting the good news that Shergar had won, and on even more occasions that the donkey they had backed had tripped over its trotters and had been shot.

These continual interruptions didn't go down at all well with the other players. Especially as the time it took Harry to inform his fellow players what he was about to do took almost as long as the journey to the bookies. He wasn't a particularly good player and found it difficult to restrain his emotions. When dealt a hand, any hand he would jump up, punch the air and yell, "Ya ya ya fffffffucker" followed by "Hhhhhit me" and very often someone did.

At the beginning, the game was full of camaraderie and bon homme but when certain players began to lose, the camaraderie went out the door.

That coupled with the antics of the one armed bandit made for an interesting spectacle. He, for obvious reasons, had great difficulty handling his cards. He had two choices, either let one of his opponents see what he was holding or perform a complicated pick up, lay down and shuffle routine which either way meant he was a certain loser. Woe betide any player who mentioned throwing his hand in. The bandit would jump up ready to punch the miscreant. Of course, as often as not when he jumped up he would drop his cards, upset the table and generally cause mayhem. This absolute debacle of a game was like no other ever encountered in any other pub. But then no other pub had such idiots.

As the day worn on the early morning members were beginning to wane. They had out sung themselves, or in most cases spent up. Had just enough Dutch courage to face the consequences of their unofficial Bank Holiday. But a combination of guilt, tiredness and vast quantities of alcohol made them grieved. It wasn't their fault that they had spent the day in the pub. It wasn't their fault that they had gambled the rent and electric money. It certainly wasn't their fault that the other players were a bunch of fucking thieving cheats and should be fucking sorted out.

That was why we had two of the biggest hardest bouncers on duty from two o'clock on a Monday afternoon.

There was always a fight at the end of the session, always someone who got barred. But such was the Monday club there was always someone to take their place next week.

# Day Out

Over the years regulars came and went with great regularity. Some you were delighted to see the back of, others you missed for a time. Now and again there were a few who left a hole in your heart, a dent in your till and you knew that no-one would take their place.

One such body was Alex. Now Alex was a grumpy bad-tempered, awkward beggar who would go out of his way to cause controversy, or an argument. He was at his happiest when he had caused mayhem and he took shit from no-one. Despite that (and those were his best features) he was one of my favourite customers.

He was an ex-cop and subsequently an ex-publican. His drinking sprees and capacity were legend but by the time I came across him he was dying.

It wasn't that Alex couldn't stop drinking, it was that he WOULDN'T. Who the hell was going to tell him what he could and couldn't do? He wouldn't be dictated to by anyone and especially regarding his own mortality. He would sit at the end of the bar dispensing vitriolic wit and advice to anyone listening and as soon as the growling had begun, off he would trot leaving arguments raging in his wake.

I had gradually noticed that the quantity he was putting away daily had significantly dropped, but figured that just possibly he was at last heeding medical advice. I should have known better. When you see someone on a daily basis the change in their appearance can go unnoticed for sometime and Alex on a good day looked hellish, so on a bad day looked pretty much the same. I did, however, get a terrible shock on the day of the village gala. After days of badgering he had been persuaded to accompany his grand-daughter to the event and, with great reluctance, attended. But twenty minutes of being told how awful he looked was too much even for him so he retreated to the bar.

One of the attractions of the Gala was a kid's face painting artist and we had a variety of mini lions, tigers, butterflies and Smurfs. When Alex and little Alexa made their entrance, I was delighted to see the old fool had entered into the spirit of the day by allowing Alexa to be transformed into a tigress and he had been turned into a greenish something, perhaps the Hulk?

The horror was, his colour wouldn't wash off. He really was yellow/green. His liver had finally given up the ghost and a few days later he was admitted to hospital.

His family knew that he would not recover but with the right medication and total abstinence he could have months rather than weeks. But they hadn't reckoned with his Lordship.

His blood levels were checked on a daily basis and from day one, although anyone looking at him could tell that he was not long for this world, his blood tests came back perfect. Therefore Alex argued that he should be allowed out as there was nothing wrong with him. This carried on over the weekend and he was furious that he was being kept in under false pretences. But guess what? Lo and behold there was another Alex ****** in hospital and, yes, you've got it. Our Alex was getting the other Alex's results. The other poor bugger nearly had a coronary. He had come in with a broken leg and been diagnosed as having couple of weeks to live!

At the end of the second week Alex was beside himself with boredom and after much persuasion he talked the occupational therapist into taking him and another inmate for a short walk. So, fully dressed and ready to go, they were some what disappointed to learn she had an emergency and would have to wait till the following morning. Not to be thwarted, off the two of them went for a leisurely stroll out to the front entrance. Never had fresh air seemed so sweet. Just as they were about to make their way back to the ward a bus heading for the village pulled up. Well, it had to be fate and without hesitation our man leapt (well not quite) on board and settled down for the hour long journey.

Of course the alarm was raised that this desperately ill patient had gone missing. As his comrade-in-arms was keeping schtum it took quite some time before his destination was discovered.

In the meantime, we had received a frantic call from someone claiming to be his wife asking if he was in the bar.

After telling this woman not to be bloody stupid, and that her joke was not at all funny as Alex would never likely enter these portals again, lo and behold who should stumble down the steps demanding a large whisky? It was the man himself. I saw no good reason to deny him his request, the damage was well and truly done. Of course it was on the house.

Within minutes the posse arrived and the bold boy was carted back to captivity and sadly he passed away the following day. The consensus of opinion was that the exertion of his escapade was too much. That, coupled with the alcohol. Yes they were probably right, but if ever anyone did it their way, Alex did!

# QUIZ ANSWERS

## Food & Drink

1 Choux
2 Goulash
3 Almond
4 Spain
5 Pastry
6 Beetroot
7 Cork
8 Fish

## Geography

1 Austria
2 Malta
3 Florence
4 Black Sea
5 Thessalonika
6 Liege
7 Switzerland
8 Germany

## Music

1    Simon Le Bon
2    Beach Boys
3    Wales
4    Tony Christie
5    Stevie Wonder
6    Boy George
7    Whitney Houston
8    Coldplay

## General Knowledge

1    Winfield.
2    The sale of British Gas shares.
3    Queenstown, Ireland (renamed Cobh in 1922)
4    On the moon.
5    Absolute zero (0 degrees Kelvin)
6    October (31 days plus one hour)
7    Mount Everest.
8    Scafell Pike (*not* Scafell which is a nearby peak)